Reputation Mana

3 Manuscripts in 1 Book, Including: Business Branding,

Social Media Marketing and Content Marketing

Santino Spencer

More by Santino Spencer

Discover all books from the Marketing Management Series by Santino Spencer at:

bit.ly/santino-spencer

Book 1: Marketing Strategy

Book 2: Business Branding

Book 3: Digital Marketing

Book 4: Social Media Marketing

Book 5: Marketing Analytics

Book 6: Content Marketing

Book 7: Business Development

Book 8: Mobile Marketing

Themed book bundles available at discounted prices:

bit.ly/santino-spencer

Copyright

Under no circumstances will any legal responsibility or blame be held against the publisher for any reparation, damages, or monetary loss due to the information herein, either directly or indirectly.

Respective authors own all copyrights not held by the publisher.

The information herein is offered for informational purposes solely, and is universal as so. The presentation of the information is without contract or any type of guaranteed assurance.

The trademarks that are used are without any consent, and the publication of the trademark is without permission or backing by the trademark owner. All trademarks and brands within this book are for clarifying purposes only and are the owned by the owners themselves, not affiliated with this document.

Table of Contents

Reputation Management... 1

More by Santino Spencer.. 2

Copyright... 3

Table of Contents.. 5

Book 1: Business Branding 8

    INTRODUCTION.. 9

    CHAPTER 1: STEP 1 - FIGURE OUT THE BRAND PURPOSE 11

    CHAPTER 2: STEP 2 - DETERMINE YOUR TARGET AUDIENCE 19

    CHAPTER 3: STEP 3 - RESEARCH YOUR BRAND'S COMPETITORS28

    CHAPTER 4: STEP 4 - PREPARE YOUR MISSION STATEMENT 35

    CHAPTER 5: STEP 5 - DEVELOP YOUR BRAND NAME AND LOGO42

    CHAPTER 6: STEP 6 - BUILD A BRAND STORY 51

    CHAPTER 7: STEP 7 - MARKET YOUR BRAND............................ 58

    CONCLUSION 66

Book 2: Social Media Marketing.. 67

    INTRODUCTION.. 68

    CHAPTER 1: STEP 1 – UNDERSTAND WHY YOUR BUSINESS
NEEDS IT 70

    CHAPTER 2: STEP 2 - MARKET RESEARCH DONE RIGHT 78

    CHAPTER 3: STEP 3 - HOW TO MARKET ON FACEBOOK 86

    CHAPTER 4: STEP 4 - HOW TO MARKET ON INSTAGRAM 93

    CHAPTER 5: STEP 5 - HOW TO MARKET ON YOUTUBE 100

    CHAPTER 6: STEP 6 - FOCUSING ON THE RIGHT NICHE MARKET107

CHAPTER 7: STEP 7 - BUILD AN UNFORGETTABLE PRESENCE . 114

CONCLUSION... 122

Book 3: Content Marketing... 124

INTRODUCTION 125

CHAPTER 1: STEP 1 - UNDERSTAND THE VALUE PROPOSITION 127

CHAPTER 2: STEP 2 - BUILD THE NARRATIVE WITH CONTENT MARKETING 134

CHAPTER 3: STEP 3 - STRUCTURE INFLUENCE AND AUTHORITY 144

CHAPTER 4: STEP 4 - BUILD AND STRATEGIZE 152

CHAPTER 5: STEP 5 - ALIGN CONTENT MARKETING WITH THE BUYER'S JOURNEY 167

CHAPTER 6: STEP 6 - APPEAL TO YOUR CUSTOMER-BASE...... 186

CHAPTER 7: STEP 7 - DISTRIBUTING YOUR CONTENT 203

CONCLUSION... 217

More by Santino Spencer 219

Book 1: Business Branding

7 Easy Steps to Master Brand Management, Reputation Management, Business Communication & Storytelling

Santino Spencer

Introduction

Welcome to *Business Branding;* whether you are trying to run a business or just up your branding game, you have made a great choice. The seven steps shared within *Business Branding* will provide great value to enhance your success. Every business, regardless of size, has to have some type of strategy for branding. Simply going about branding without a plan can be very costly and honestly might even hurt your brand.

The following chapters will discuss every detail of business branding. If you want your customers to identify your brand accurately, you need more than just a name and a logo. These two things are undoubtedly very important, but there is more to branding than just that, and we are going to explain it to you in a seven-step process.

When branding is done properly, it sets your brand apart from all other competitors in the market, and you get a loyal group of customers who truly believe in your brand. Developing your brand identity and ensuring that it remains constant across all platforms is one of the first steps of business branding. Once you are done with the basics, you have to look into brand marketing and reputation management. Your customer service also has to remain top-notch.

For a beginner, all of these things might seem overwhelming, and that is why this guide will be helpful, to carve out a path for you that you simply need to follow. The biggest asset of any successful company is the brand, and so, you need to pay attention to every detail while building yours. Let's get started.

Chapter 1: Step 1 - Figure Out the Brand Purpose

The first step to branding your business is to figure out the purpose of your brand. It is a very important step; however, most organizations overlook this step simply because they fail to understand what it's about and its benefits. If you take some time to understand what brand purpose is all about and how it can benefit your brand management, it would be super valuable for you. Creating a strong brand purpose will not only separate you from your competitors but also give you authority and greater meaning. This becomes even more important when you attempt to market to Gen Z.

The way the market works is constantly being changed by conscious customers and generation Z who see brand purpose as an important aspect while choosing the service or product they want to purchase. A study conducted by Edelman in 2017 known as the 'Earned Brand Study' revealed that almost fifty percent of consumers all over the world think of themselves as belief-driven buyers and almost sixty-seven percent of them purchased a service or a brand because they agreed with the brand's views on a controversial matter. This shows that what sets a brand or company apart from its competitors is a strong brand purpose.

What Is a Brand Purpose?

A brand purpose can be defined as the reason for the brand's existence beyond making money. It is the reason for the activities of the organization or brand. The brand purpose of a company is based on the company's beliefs and the differences it believes it can make in the world. Even though it doesn't have to be about saving the planet, it should be sufficient to some extent. For instance, by undertaking actions, those are small yet meaningful.

Brand purpose should, however, not be confused with 'brand promise'. Something that provides the buyer with an indication about what to expect from a service or product is known as 'brand promise,' whereas the brand purpose of a service or product goes well beyond that. It helps to form a connection between the buyer and the company on a more emotional level.

There is no need for a connection between the brand promise and the brand purpose as a brand purpose generally focuses primarily on the reason for the brand's existence. In a similar way, brand purpose is different from social purpose, although they have certain similarities. This can be clarified by saying that a brand purpose revolves around initiatives that are product-led and strive to simultaneously benefit society and achieving business.

In addition to the previously mentioned, the brand's purpose should also not be confused with the brand's vision, mission, and value. These terms don't mean the same, even though they are related to one another. The foundation of a business is known as its purpose, while the remaining three form its building blocks. A brand's value is the ethical clock of the brand that helps it move in the right direction in order to achieve its goal. It describes how the brand should behave while it's moving to fulfill its vision. The brand's mission is the method or procedure it uses to achieve its goals, while a brand's vision is the set of goals it wants to achieve.

How to Build a Brand Purpose?

In order to know your brand purpose, it's important that you ask yourself a few questions like: What is the reason behind the existence of your brand or organization? What is the long-term purpose of the brand or organization? Is it to improve the society as it is today? When you are able to find answers to these questions, you will be able to figure out the brand's intent of being.

Here are a few ways by which you can develop your own brand purpose:

- ***Put Your Customer First*** – For proper brand management, the brand purpose of an organization should always have its customers ahead of other things. This implies that the consumer should be put at the forefront of every step taken and every decision made. Your brand purpose is what makes you relatable to your chosen audience. It needs to attract your key demographic even though it might not resonate with all customers.

- *Think for the Long Term* – Your brand purpose needs to be embedded within and without the image of your brand and its practice. It cannot simply be a one-off marketing strategy. This implies that the consumers need to see the organizations carrying out their brand purpose instead of just doing a one-off stunt.

- *Have a Clear Idea About the Purpose of Your Brand and the Reason Behind Your Actions* – Your brand purpose should be associated with the reason for the organization's being. In addition to that, it should also be the reason why the organization sells a particular product. It is also part and parcel of everything that happens in the organization. This purpose should be present right from the start. If you simply add a purpose to a product that has already been established so that it complies with a particular set of rules or criteria, the buyers will see right through it. A brand purpose needs to be established at the start. Even if it isn't, there should at least be something that the organization or company has developed gradually over time.

- ***Differentiate Your CSR From Your Brand Purpose*** – Even though CSR or corporate social responsibility is important and needs to be advertised worldwide, it is still different from brand purpose. The brand purpose of a company should be associated with the items or services it is selling or providing. As a way of donating some free time and energy for a good purpose, a fancy car company can offer to clean the neighborhood for free. However, this does not convey anything meaningful regarding the actual item the company is selling. In a similar manner, brand purpose is not the same as philanthropy. A company can donate a large sum of money for a charitable cause; however, this does not convey any details about the product the company is selling.

Advantages of Having a Strong Brand Purpose

Some of the important benefits of having a brand purpose are:

- A brand purpose that is unique can help distinguish your brand from the other competitors.
- It can help construct a better emotional relationship between the brand and its customers. This, in turn, will help in increasing loyalty and sales as well.
- The brand purpose of a company adds value to the lives of its consumers as well as society as a whole.

Importance of Having a Brand Purpose

In recent times, all companies and organizations know what product they are selling, a few of them also know how to do it (for instance, with the help of a creative ad campaign, a fun packaging design, a clear brand differentiation strategy, etc.), however, only some of the organizations actually know why they are doing it (for example, as Dove does it to assist people in accepting their bodies and feeling good about themselves). An organization will be able to create deeper emotional relationships with everyone, including their stakeholders, investors, employees, and consumers, when its employees can give an answer to the question "Why are we here?"

In today's world, employees need to understand their actual motive behind working for a particular company, and consumers require products and brands that instill a real meaning in their lives. Organizations and brands are required to represent their products as well as the people behind those products.

Here are some of the reasons why it's important to have a good brand purpose:

- *It Increases Engagement* – While everyone wants to change the world for the better, some people don't really understand how or where to start. If, in such a situation, they find out about an organization or brand that would help them make a difference in the world with the help of their products, consumers will be elated to contribute. Having a strong brand purpose can, thus, help brands interact with more people who would want to spend their money on things that could help them make a difference in the world.

- *It Conveys That the Organization Cares About More Than Just Money* – If an organization has a good brand purpose, it shows the consumers that the organization offers more than just tangible offerings. It lets its consumers know that the organization cares about more than simply making a monetary profit. This is extremely important because nowadays, people are searching for brands and organizations that are willing to make a positive effect on the world by taking action against the wrongdoings. Nowadays, organizations use several strategies like blogs, email newsletters, social media marketing, brand activation, and CSR projects to convey their message and purpose.

- *It Makes the Organization More Appealing to the Consumers* – If a company has a strong brand purpose, it appeals more to the consumers as it makes them feel like they are helping to make a difference in the world. It helps make them feel as if they are a part of something bigger. Consumers want to work with brands that think about society as well as the environment. Thus, brand purpose is extremely important.

Examples of Brand Purpose

Here are a few examples of strong brand purposes:

- *The Body Shop: products that enrich biodiversity, promote environmental sustainability, and raise awareness about abusive relationships.*

  The Body Shop has transformed its stores into hubs for social activists in order to bring its brand purpose to life and support gender equality.

- *Innocent: Promoting community and sustainability.*

  Their campaigns reflect their brand values, and they appear to be exactly as they are: innocent. Consumers feel like they can trust the brand as its promotions are simple, loveable, and cute.

- *Dove: Improving self-esteem and discovering the value of "real beauty."*

  They encourage women to embrace their natural bodies and be kinder to themselves through their #speakbeautiful movement. Dove impacts the world by making their brand more 'human' and relatable.

In conclusion, a brand purpose should be a genuine display of what the brand's target consumers hold dear and should show a real desire for positive social impact.

Chapter 2: Step 2 - Determine Your Target Audience

There is always a big risk associated with launching a new service, product, or business into the market. If you know the market landscape, it could help you focus on your marketing strategies and also minimize that risk. One of the most important aspects of formulating a market strategy for branding your business in such a way that it is cost-effective is by identifying the right target audience for your business. If your marketing strategy is broad right from the start, it would not be as successful as one that has a targeted market segment or highly niche. Thus, you need to determine your target audiences before you start your marketing efforts for brand management.

However, targeting a specific market does not suggest that you need to eliminate others who don't fulfill your list of criteria. The good thing about having a target audience is that it allows you to convey your message to the right group of people who are most likely to purchase your products or services. With a proper understanding of how to determine your target audience, you can earn more and spend less by reaching the most important leads in your network.

What Do You Mean by Target Audience?

A target audience can be defined as a particular group of consumers who are most likely to react positively to the services, products, and promotions of your brand or business. You need to understand the reason behind dividing your list of would-be traffic before beginning to browse through the kinds of target audience or making a list of your target audience. It forms a large part of business communication. Your analysis of the target audience is often based on several factors income, age, location, etc. For example, if you own a make-up company, you might want to attract people who live in a region you can ship your products to and who can afford your products.

Why Do You Need a Target Audience?

Determining a target audience becomes essential because the information, language, and channels that you use to communicate with your audience might be effective for one demographic and ineffective for another. Figuring out your target audience will help you to develop a tone that will help you connect with your customers and speak with them. It will help guide you towards a better marketing strategy and increase consistency in your messaging, and this will help you to create stronger relationships with your consumers.

Moreover, if you understand how your customers pick and compare products, it can help you improve and adjust your marketing campaigns so that you can make it more appealing to them. You will also be able to modify your value proposition if you know what your customers want. This will help make your brand more relatable to a particular problem or need. You would be able to modify your SEO and keyword strategies if you knew how your consumers talk. You will also be able to know what people want from your brand and where to find your target audience.

Ultimately, the most important thing about creating a target audience profile is building relevancy. You are more likely to gain a customer if the products you present and the things you offer matches with what your customers are looking for, whereas you will be making it difficult for yourself to connect with your consumers on a deeper level if the consumer you are searching for is just "everybody." Remember that when you connect with a customer on a deeper level, it's more likely that the customer will turn into a loyal customer and an advocate for your business.

Types of Target Audience

Brand management is all about figuring out who your target audience is. To figure it out you need to look at their features and personalities and then create a user persona that will help you to differentiate one customer from another. It will help you to refine your audience. However, you can start by defining some of the important aspects that you need to know regarding your audience.

Here are a few types of target audience profiles that you can look into:

- ***Target Audience Profile Driven by Personalities*** – Personality is an important aspect of an effective marketing strategy, and it is something that you should always include in your campaigns. You should always consider the things that are valuable to your customer and the things that aren't when you are wondering about how to figure out your target audience. Try to find out which issues your customers care about, how they spend their free time, etc. For example, if you desire to connect with the GenZ or millennial audience that gives importance to social issues, you might want to show off your ethical side more.

- ***A Local or Geographical Target Audience Profile*** – Only a very small number of brands can afford to target consumers from all around the world. When your scope is that large, it gets very hard to earn attention from people. In addition to that, you might not be able to provide your products and services to consumers from each and every country anyway. Figure out how to connect with new customers locally unless you can offer digital services. Figure out the maximum distance to which you can deliver your products, and how far you can afford to go to provide your services.

- *A Target Audience Profile Based on Age* – People belong to different age groups behave in different ways. Interestingly, the person you target isn't always the person who is most likely to purchase your product. For example, when you are preparing a target audience analysis for a newborn, your target audience would be the parents of a newborn instead of the babies. Try to keep the range of your target audience as narrow as you can if you don't know the actual age-range of your customers. For example, begin by searching for the most probable ages of CEOs in the industry when you are selling enterprise-level software. Through this method, you can create promotional strategies that attract the correct age-range.

There are different kinds of target audience present in the world. The market for a particular brand is often unique to that particular business as every business has a one-of-a-kind sales strategy, a different purpose, and a different set of values. Apart from the factors given before, you might also need to combine several different characteristics to get an effective user persona. Therefore, remember to look at:

- Buying concerns
- Gender
- Motivation for buying
- Favorite websites
- Language

- The social media platforms they use
- Problems and concerns
- Needs and aspirations
- Relationship or family status
- Job title or income

Tips for Identifying the Right Target Audience

It's not easy to find your unique target audience. To have an impact on your bottom line, your target audience analysis should be focused and in-depth. This implies that you cannot simply decide to market your products to mothers in New York. You have to decide whether you are going to market to working mothers who have children below the age of five and fall in the age group of thirty to fifty. Your inbound marketing strategies will become more effective, the more precise you get.

Here are a few tips to help you identify the most profitable target audience for your products:

- ***Conduct Market Research*** – Analyze the different aspects of the market first by conducting proper market research. You can do this by performing a SWOT analysis. This will help you identify the strengths and weaknesses of the business as well as its threats and opportunities. This kind of market research will help you identify:

- Competition
- Motivations
- Pain points and personality types (persona)
- Buying habits of the customers
- Economic shifts
- Market trends
- Industries (non-profit, lighting, accounting, medical)
- Psychographics (behavior, attitude, personality, lifestyle, hobbies, values)
- Demographics (marital status, income level, occupation, gender, age)
- Location (international, national, or local)

An important first step to figuring out the right target audience is by understanding which factors contribute to your market.

- ***Know the Purchase Path and Pain Points*** – It is crucial to pay attention to defining your target customers as a part of your market research. In addition to that, you should also know what they think about purchase path and pain points. You could approach this by asking yourself pertinent questions and thinking like the customers. You could ask yourself questions like:

  - What does my target audience want to achieve?
  - How can I give a solution to their problems?

By thinking about the answers to these problems, you can craft personas as well as frame content that answers the problems surrounding the stages of the purchasing cycle (decision, consideration, and awareness). Crafting personas will help you understand the pain points and needs of your customers. Content and messages that are tailored to speak to specific personas will increase the chances of shifting them down the sales funnel.

- *Employ Multi-Segmented Marketing Strategies* – This strategy can help you gain customers from various segments of the market to purchase the same services or products for the same purposes. There might be different decision-makers who would get separate messages; however, they will also contribute to the sale or purchase. While some brands and businesses offer various product lines that appeal to unique groups of customers, others offer the same product to more than a single segment.

- *Know Your Existing Customers* – Learning everything regarding your existing customers, including their preferences, demographics, etc., is one of the best methods of identifying the perfect target audience for your business. You can explore different avenues, including:

    o Gather extensive information about user responses by using tools such as Facebook Insights, HubSpot, Hotjar, Google Analytics, etc.

o   Inspecting your website and social media analytics. With the help of this method, you can find out which website pages customers are visiting the most, who is visiting your site, and how they are navigating it. In addition to that, you will also get to understand who is communicating with your social media networks.

Nowadays, understanding your target audience is considered one of the most effective methods of surviving in the current marketplace. You can't afford to use a generalized marketing approach in a world where consumers are expecting to get unique and personalized experiences from businesses.

Chapter 3: Step 3 - Research Your Brand's Competitors

While branding your business, researching your brand's competitors is one of the primary activities that you must perform. Competitive research is a key tool for brand management. Competitive research helps you to get ideas about the ongoing trends in the market. Once you can identify the current trends, it will be easier to predict future movements as well. Customers will buy your product if it serves their purpose. If you notice that customers are choosing your competitors over you, it means that their products serve the customers better than yours.

Competitive research also allows you to have an insight into your competitors' strategies, insights, goals, and achievements. Then after thorough research, you can bring changes to your products accordingly and certainly expect a better outcome. One of the most important benefits of competitive research for brand management is that it allows you to discover the gaps present in the market. You can identify potential places in the market where no competitor has started to serve yet. You can grab the opportunity to fill in the gaps and 3establish your brand. The most important tool for brand management is that you need a full-proof plan, which you can only have once you have acquired all the required data. Only then can you plan a powerful and legitimate strategy for successfully branding your business.

Let us discuss the important steps for successful research of your brand's competitors.

Identify Your Direct Competitors

Direct competitors are the ones who offer the same services or products to the customers as your company. They directly operate at the segment of the market where you target to operate as well. Therefore your target audiences are also the same. Identify your direct competitors and create company information cards for each one of them. This should contain a detailed description of the company and its business, the company's market share and sales trend, the buyer personas, the year it was founded, the annual revenue of the company, etc. In this way, you can have a thorough understanding of your competitor's strategy and current position in the market. This will help you to strategize your business product accordingly to make it a bigger hit.

Identify Your Indirect Competitors

If you think that you only need to identify your direct competitors, then you are completely wrong. This is where most people go wrong. You also need to identify your indirect competitors, i.e., the brands and companies that don't directly operate in the same segment of the market as yours. They may not offer the same service or product as you, but their product may satisfy your customers, thereby reducing your sale. For example, different food chains that don't offer the same kinds of food, but if one gains more popularity, it can suppress the other chains. The same goes for the clothing industry, the beauty industry, and so on. It is very important to keep these competitors on your radar because they can enter your competitive zone anytime, so it is vital to keep a close watch on them along with your direct competitors. The market is always changing, so it is very important to perform competitive analysis regularly to get ahead in the rat race.

Identify Future Competitors

There are potential future competitors in every segment of the market. They are mainly bigger brands that can suddenly change the entire market by using their superior powers and strong strategies. One such example is how the online clothing and grocery platforms are surpassing the offline retails and grocery stores. If you are aware of your potential future competitors, you will be able to pre-plan all the necessary precautions and changes that you need to make to ensure that you don't fall behind.

Focus on the Products Offered by Your Competitors

The service or product is the heart of any business out there. This is what makes a business unique. This is something that you should keep a close watch on. You need to have detailed information about the service or product offered by your competitors, the services they are offering, and the quality of that service or product. Make sure to check their prices and if they are offering any discounts to their customers or not. Some key points that you need to keep a check on are: the way they distribute their services or products, how are they different from their competitors, the different pricing strategies they use for brick and mortar versus online purchase, the needs and characteristics of their targeted customers, their market share, their working strategies, etc.

Analyze Your Competitors' Sales Strategies and Their Results

Keep a note on the involvement of the salesperson in the product, how frequently do they offer discounts to their products, how much revenue do they generate or what is the total sales volume, are they losing any customer or not, and if so then why, their reselling partners, whether they are scaling down or expanding, their locations and the advantages because of those, their selling channels, sales processes, etc. This information will help you to have a thorough understanding of their sales strategies and tactics. Thus you will be able to bring changes in your sales strategies to compete with them.

In the case of publicly held companies, you will get the information online, but in the case of private companies, you will need to do some digging. You can reach out to their customers and try to gather some information about them. The most important information that you need to take from their customer is what made them choose them over you, i.e., how are they better than you. You need to find what is the most attractive point about them, which makes people chose them. Gather honest feedback about your product's services. Try to know the things that people find the most appealing in your product and the things that are pushing them away. By knowing these, you will be able to bring necessary changes in your services for building your brand.

Analyze Your Competitors' Marketing Strategies

Checking your competitors' websites is the best way to keep track of their marketing strategies and tactics. Keep a check on their offline and online marketing campaigns, published data sheets and buying guides, case studies, media kit, press releases, featured articles, FAQ section, slide decks, cartoons and infographics (if used), podcasts (if any), webinars, videos, e-books, blogs. Check them regularly to keep yourself updated.

Know Their Content Strategy

Check the quantity of their content. Knowing how much content they post and how many times they post, you can have a rough idea of their content quantity. How frequently they post content is also a very important point to look at. Are they posting weekly or a monthly basis, are some of the points you should examine. If you find loads of content, it probably means that your competitors are posting regularly. By going through those contents, you can have a rough idea of their strategies for generating leads. Then you should examine the quality of the contents they provide. If their content quality is not up to the mark, then no matter how frequently they post, it is of no use. Pick a handful of samples and go through them instead of going through every single one. It will make things easier and manageable.

While analyzing your competitors' content, keep a check on the attached bio in the samples, the writers of the contents, are they providing free contents or are charging money to view them, are the contents easy to read i.e., are there adequate use of bulletins, the writing tone, depth of the contents, grammatical or spelling mistakes, the accuracy of the contents. Also, keep a check on the illustrations, images, and infographics used. Try to know whether they are recruiting external graphic designers for those or are getting it done by in-house members only. When you finally have a thorough understanding of your competitors' marketing tactics, it will be easier for you to find out what is working best for them and what are their strong points. For defeating someone, you need to first identify their strong points.

Analyze Your Competitors' Content Engagement

For analyzing your competitors' content engagement, you need to check how the audiences respond to their posted content. Check the number of likes, shares, and comments on their posts. Keep a check on how they categorize their posts (if they use tags or not), how they promote on social media, where do the readers react the most (i.e., are they getting more engagement in Facebook or some other platform). Take notes on the topics that get re-tweeted the most. Find out whether the comments are mostly negative or positive. By looking at these points, you will be able to judge their contents from the audience's point of view and understand clearly what the audiences like and what they don't like.

Run A SWOT Analysis

Along with analyzing your competitors' marketing strategies, sales strategies, and business strategies, you also need to perform a SWOT analysis. SWOT analysis involves the analysis of your competitors' threats, opportunities, weaknesses, and strengths. Check the opportunities identified by your competitors' in the market, the threats they are facing, where they need improvement (i.e., their weaknesses), whether your company has an advantage over them, and where they have an advantage over your company. This will help you to have an overall fair comparison of your company with theirs. This will help you to find out where do you exactly stand in the market presently. Try comparing your competitors' weaknesses to your strengths and check whether you can use it for your benefit or not.

Chapter 4: Step 4 - Prepare Your Mission Statement

A mission statement of a business can come in several forms. Do you promise to keep the needs of your consumers first or to create intuitive technology, innovative applications, or quality products? Statements can run many paragraphs or be only a sentence.

A mission statement can be defined as a simple statement that describes the goals and values of a business. It forms a summary of what your business is willing to do for its owners, employees, and customers. It focuses on why your company functions the way it does and how it does it. A few mission statements also expand themselves and include the fourth and fifth dimensions. For example, what the company is willing to do for its community and the world as a whole. A meaningful mission statement can, therefore, provide its employees and team members a common goal to work towards, provide potential directions for growth in the future, and also set a company apart from its competitors.

When you are preparing a mission statement for your business for the first time or revising an old one, it gives you an opportunity to define the culture, ethics, goals, and norms for the company's decision-making. Sometimes, refreshing the mission statement of your company can help you take a step back and rethink the most important purpose of your business.

However, don't bother to include a mission statement if it won't help you guide your business communication or be useful for your brand management. Just because a traditional business plan generally includes one, it's not a good enough reason for you to include it as well. A vast majority of mission statements are generally meaningless jargon that uses high-sounding, vague phrases that can be used to describe any business. You don't have to write a mission statement simply because some experts or checklist recommended you.

How to Create a Strong Mission Statement?

You could include a mission statement if you want to get your customers, investors, and employees to understand what your business stands for and adds clarity to your business goals. It is an art to be able to craft a mission statement that is so impactful that your customers will laud it, and your staff will adopt it.

Here are some strategies by which you can develop a mission statement:

- ***Begin with a Story That Defines the Market*** – Even though you don't have to include a story in your mission statement, you should think about it carefully. This is because storytelling can help guide you when you create your mission statement. For instance, suppose you are the customer who is trying to decide whether to purchase the products you sell or not. Try to use your imagination to understand how purchasing from you benefits her, how she finds you, and why she wants a particular product. It'll be better if your story is more concrete.

A good market-defining story describes the want, the need, or the reason for buying a product. It should describe the persona of the buyer or the target customer as well as how your company is unique or differs from most other companies. It can be simplified by thinking about what a business doesn't do or what it isn't. Even though it does not form a part of the mission statement, you must have it in your mind when you are creating your mission statement. Create a quick list of what your business does and does not do if you are having difficulty getting started.

- *Define Your Purpose* – A good way to begin your mission statement is by mentioning the good you do. Figure out what makes your business special by using your market-defining story. You don't need to stop global warming or cure cancer to be doing something good. So, don't undervalue your company. For instance, you are doing something good even if you are providing trustworthy auto repair in your neighborhood through your unique policies, which are narrowed down to your specialty.

Similarly, you are also doing good work if you are providing excellent-quality food (that emphasizes local and organic items) in your neighborhood at a premium price. This forms a very important part of your mission statement. You can also include something that your business is doing for the betterment of the world. However, the claims about doing something good for the world should be different from any other companies and needs to be meaningful. You can include the terms "green" or "clean" only if it is true, and you maintain it meticulously. If it's not always true or isn't important, you don't need to say it in your mission statement.

- *Include What Your Company Does for Its Employees* – For a business to last, it has to be good towards their employees as well. As compared to turnover, keeping employees turns out to be better for the bottom line. The culture of the company matters, and so does motivate and rewarding its employees. You can include what your business provides for its employees in your mission statement. It is recommended by experts that you should define it here instead of just asserting how it's good for the employees and then make it true forever after. Qualities such as empowerment, tools, training, respect for creativity and ideas, diversity, fairness, and the like are really important.

However, you have to work hard to make a difference and create a way by which the generalized goals appear more specific and concrete because almost every company at least says that they give priority to those things. There's a built-in dilemma with this part of the mission statement. Even though it's good for everyone, if you include it in the mission statement, it is quite difficult to do that without having to state what every other company states. It is probably a good idea to state that you value respect for diversity, a creative and healthy work environment, training, room to grow, and fair compensation even if that part of your mission statement is not different from others. That is because it can also serve as a lever for self-enforcement and a reminder for the workers, supervisors, and owners. If your business is friendly to remote virtual workplaces or families, or if you have a special view about your relationship with the employees, include that in your mission statement.

- *Discuss, Digest, Edit, and Review* – Strong mission statements live for a long time, define objectives, and serve several functions. Therefore, this step is a must. You can begin by using a customer-facing subset for general publication and creating a full mission statement for internal usage. Several businesses also divide their mission statements into segments and set aside the segments, and categorize them by their goals or types. You can use sections or bullet points if you want. Keep a sharp eye out for hype and buzzwords while editing and remove any part that does not specifically apply to our business.

You can, however, include special elements occasionally that can act as long-term reminders and rules. Phrases like "great customer service," "world-class," and "being the best possible" don't mean much since everyone uses them as well. Make sure that you have a belief in what you are writing. Then, you can show your draft to others and ask for their insights. Listen to their opinions and edit accordingly. Change is constant. So, your mission statement should never be written in stone. Review and revise it as necessary.

Why Is a Mission Statement Important?

Mission statements can be very beneficial for brand management. Here are a few reasons why companies need to have a clear, written mission statement:

- *Encouraging Critical Thinking* – Mission statements allow people to think about how their actions will influence the goals of the business in both the short and the long term. It would help people think about how the business could evolve in various contexts while upholding the values of the business. Having a clear mission statement is essential as it conveys a brief philosophy and strategy that could be applicable to any situation within a business.

- **_Envisioning the Future_** – A mission statement helps direct the growth of a business and provides an ideal vision for the future of the organization. They help encourage its employees to think about how their actions will influence positive company culture and future business success. They can significantly impact the futures of the people within the company since they direct the actions of the employees.

- **_Improving Performance_** – Mission statements help set a clear goal for its employees and can thus help boost their performance. A good mission statement helps create an environment that motivates its employees to hold high standards for themselves and produce high-quality work as well. It helps motivate them to work harder towards the long-term plans of the company and promote its growth. When the employees read the mission statement, it will let them engage with the core values of the company and apply those ideas to their work.

A mission statement is thus, a declaration of what makes a company important and different from its competitors. It should be unique, achievable, strategic, encouraging, and persuasive.

Chapter 5: Step 5 - Develop Your Brand Name and Logo

As an independent business owner, one of the most challenging things you will face while branding your business is while creating a brand name and logo for your company. Creating a logo and deciding a brand name are important phases of brand management. Creating an eye-catching logo is not an easy thing to do. Similarly, giving an outshining brand name to your company is also a hectic job to do. A lot of things depend on this, so you can't be careless. Just an appealing design is not going to make your logo outshine others. Similarly, just a fancy name is not enough for keeping it as a brand name.

Brand management is all about the message you want to convey to your audience and the emotional response to a brand, and the offerings of the brand. It also includes the opinions of the customers about that particular brand. Branding your business is all about expectations, storytelling, customer-brand relationships, and remembrances. Let us discuss the brand name and logo in detail.

What Is a Brand Name?

Your brand's name is the first thing that will help your customers to identify your product and differentiate it from others. It is important to choose a brand name carefully since it beholds the key theme of any product in an economical and efficient manner. The brand name must be easily noticeable and should have such a meaning which can get easily stored in the memory and also can get easily triggered in the memory. Before deciding on a brand name, you need to perform a lot of research. It is not compulsory for a brand name to be associated to the product itself. It can be related to any people, animals, places, etc., which are somehow related to the product. In some cases, the company name is used for all the products offered by them.

The Purpose of a Brand Name

The brand name is almost like a signature that offers credit to the creator or owner of a particular service or product. The brand name is something that sets your work apart from all the other brands. The two main purposes of a brand name are verification and identification.

- *Verification:* Brand name helps to authenticate that your service or product is good and genuine.
- *Identification:* Brand name is used to identify or differentiate your brand from all the other brands who are in the same field as yours.

Requirements of A Good Brand Name

A good and impactful brand name must have the following features:

1. The brand name should be distinctive or unique.

2. The brand name should be extendable.

3. Pronouncing, identifying, and memorizing the brand name should be easy.

4. By hearing a brand's name, a person should get an idea about the benefits and qualities offered by the product.

5. The brand name should get converted into other languages easily.

6. The brand name should be eligible for registration and legal protection. The brand name should suggest the service or product category.

7. The concrete qualities of your product should be indicated by your brand's name.

8. The brand name should not project any wrong or bad meanings in any other category.

How to Select a Proper Brand Name?

1. At first, you need to define the objectives of the branding on the basis of six different criteria. They are fanciful, arbitrary, classical, compound, suggestive, and descriptive. It is very crucial to understand the role of your brand in the branding strategy of the corporate. It is also crucial to understand the relation of your brand with other products and brands. It is also very important to realize the role of your brand in the niche market as well as in the whole marketing program.

2. Generate multiple names from various potential sources such as professional consultants and agencies, potential or current customers, employees, management, and organization.

3. Screen your brand's name based on the marketing considerations and branding objectives to obtain a more synchronized list of names. Make sure that your brand's name meets all the legal requirements, can be pronounced easily, doesn't have any connotations, etc.

4. When you have a list of finalized names, begin to gather more and more detailed information on each one of the names. Then run an international legal search on them.

5. Perform consumer research for confirming the management expectations for the meaningfulness and remembrance of the brand names. The price, promotion, and the features of the product should be portrayed to the customers in such a way that they truly understand the real purpose of the brand name and also the way it will be used. You can show actual packages or animated TV commercials to give the consumers a better insight into the product.

6. You must survey various types of consumers based on the involved niche market.

7. After following the previous steps, the management can finally fix a brand's name, which will maximize the company's marketing objectives and branding.

What Is a Logo?

Logos are shapes, texts, images, or a combination of all these three things, which portrays the purpose and the name of a business. A logo is like an identification symbol for a brand. If the logo is designed brilliantly, it can also convey the story of your company and convey the brand's message to the audience. This can help to build a strong emotional bond between the brand and its target audience.

What Is the Purpose of a Logo?

There are various reasons as to why a logo is beneficial. Let us discuss some of its purposes.

- Logos encourage brand loyalty.
- Logos are responsible for storytelling, i.e., they responsible for conveying your brand's vision and mission to your audience.
- Logos set your brand apart from your competitors and make you unique.
- Logos offer a symbol to your audience, which makes them remember your brand.
- Logo ensures that your brand becomes able to make its own unique identity.
- If your brand's logo is attractive, then it will have a great first impression among your audience, thus inviting more and more customers to your business.

Constituents of a Logo

When you are going to start a business, creating your brand logo must be of utmost priority. There are various elements that constitute a logo. Let us see those.

- *Color:* Colors are not just for giving aesthetic appeals. They are much more than that. They are the ones who are mainly responsible for communicating the story you want to tell your audience. They allow your audience to understand whether you are timeless or cutting edge, wholesome or innovative, serious or playful, etc. The color palette of your logo can be made of several colors or even a single color. It is recommended that you go for a 2 to 3 color combination to make it more impactful. Make sure to choose your colors wisely because they will have a direct impact on the branding materials which you will create next.

- *Typography:* Typography is not just about the font. There is much more to it. The letters, the designs, the arrangements, everything is a part of typography. There are various examples of business logos that are built around just the name of the brand or even just a letter. Typography, if used correctly, can have a huge impact on your business' logo and branding.

- *Image:* An image can be of a simple symbol or even a detailed illustration. It can be a symbol, an icon, or can be a picture representing a value that you stand for, or maybe a thing that you sell. If you want to insert an image to your logo, then make sure that the image looks scalable and clear because it will frequently need to be resized based on where it is laced.

- *Tagline:* Tagline is basically a phrase or a sentence specially designed to make your audience hooked to your brand. It is also sometimes helpful to give the audience a rough idea about the purpose of your brand. Taglines are not always necessary for a logo. But you should consider creating a tagline when your logo alone is somewhat an abstract interpretation of a concept you want to convey.

What Makes a Logo Unique?

- *Must Be Appropriate to the Audience:* A logo doesn't need to be the flashiest in order to be the best. The main thing to consider while making a logo is that the audience should be able to relate to the logo. It is a powerful logo if it resonates with your target audience. Always remember that the logos are not only responsible for representing your brand, but it is also responsible for representing the people you speak. For example, you can't use a bright neon color when you are conveying something related to old age. Similarly, you will not be able to use muted colors when it is something concerning the kids.

- ***Must Be Easily Readable:*** Although it applies to each and every design style, this point is the most applicable for the logos that contain texts. If your audience faces difficulty in figuring out what is written, then they are likely to lose interest in your brand, and eventually, they will go away. Always make sure that your logo is very much understandable just at a single glance.

- ***Must Be Unique:*** You can always look for inspirations and references in the market industry, but make sure that our logo doesn't resemble any of the existing logos. Your goal is to create your brand's unique identity. The first step towards that is to create a unique logo that will readily set you apart from the other brands. Your brand logo should be easily differentiated from all the other logos. It should be something that is memorable, i.e., gets imprinted on your audience's head so that they can't forget it. This is the way to make your audience remember you, and if your audience remembers you, they are likely to stay loyal to you as well.

- ***Must Be Scalable:*** Your logo is going to be displayed across various media channels in different sizes, so it is important that it is clear, prominent, and scalable. Versatile logos are the best because they can be easily scaled and can be fitted into any branding need efficiently.

Chapter 6: Step 6 - Build a Brand Story

If you see carefully, every brand has a unique brand story. It is very important for a brand to have its own story for establishing an emotional connection between the brand and the audience.

What Is a Brand Story?

A brand story is a narrative that comprises the feelings and facts created by your business or brand. It is very much different from TV commercials. TV commercials only focus on the brand and what it has to offer, whereas brand stories are mainly inspirational stories that demand an emotional connection from its viewers. Things that can have an influence on your brand are what people say about you, location, values, purpose, in-store experience, marketing, quality, history, price, product, etc. Brand storytelling has been there for ages, but it has got a new dimension since the rise of social media.

Brand's marketing blogs, people's reactions to them, everything becomes a part of the brand story. Because of the huge influence of social media, you can't take full control of your brand story, but you can always have a lead. You can insert your engaging and compelling story. You can make it authentic ad true to your own values. When you add your own voice to your brand story, it is going to clarify your mission and is going to help you to build an emotional bond with your audience.

Advantages of Having a Brand Story

- ***Helps You to Stand Out:*** What do you think makes you unique from others? You may think it's the product features or designs. But the actual thing that sets you apart from all your competitors is your unique brand story. There are various similar products in the market, so if you really want to stand out, you need to go out there and share your story to let people know why and how you are different from everyone else. The most important aspects of your brand's story are your struggles, challenges, and journey. You may think that people are not interested in them much as they are self-indulgent, but you are wrong.

   People do want to know where you came from, where did you learn to work, what motivated you, what tried to stop you, how you coped with struggles, etc. It is satisfying as well as beneficial to share your own story with your audience. Letting them know about why you do what you do is the best thing you can do to form an emotional bond with them. With storytelling, you can even lay emphasis on the things that make you and your content unique and can outshine all your competitors easily.

- ***Helps to Humanize Your Brand:*** People want to get close to people who have humanity. None of us want to get close to heartless folks. If you share your story of struggles and emotions and happiness, they will understand that you are someone with a warm heart. It can be a great plus point when it comes to winning the trust of your audience. Most brands make a common mistake in emphasizing the product's services and features while sharing their story. They don't even realize what opportunity they are missing out on. Sharing your brand's story is the best way to cultivate emotional bonds, build transparency, and reduce gaps between your brand and the audience.

- ***Helps You to Attract the Right Group of People:*** We all have witnessed damages done by numerous companies around us. This has forced people to not engage with brands or companies that don't offer consideration and care to people. This not only goes for the consumers but is also applicable for potential employees. Brand storytelling not only tells people about what you do but also gives people an idea about what your values are and what you believe, and what your aspirations are. When you are vocal about your values and thoughts, people find it much easier to get themselves aligned with you. You can then easily find many talented people who will love to work for you. This is because when you pitch about your values, people will understand the kind of people they will be working for, which will make them more inclined towards securing a job.

- *Helps You to Convey Your Value:* While competing as a brand, you need to keep two things as your weapon: values and price. Competition on price is never-ending because there is always going to be something cheaper than your product. There can always be a small, scrappier team that will offer things cheaper than yours, even if their quality is a disaster. There are always a certain amount of customers who only cares about the price and will always go for the cheaper one regardless of the quality of the product. But if you compete on the values, then you have a fair chance to stay in the game. The value that you add to your product, the satisfied customer experience, etc. are the ones that are going to make you win the game.

- *Saves You from Rumours:* In this age of social media, transparency is the key. You can use it to your benefit, or it can even ruin you. If you don't take charge of yourself and share your story, people are going to make their own versions and spread rumors. So, it is better to design your own story rather than falling victim to rumors.

How to Build a Brand Story?

Let us discuss some of the key elements that you need to keep in mind if you want to build a compelling brand story to tell your audience.

- ***Stop Telling, Start Showing:*** Showing has a better impact rather than telling. You are more likely to get convinced by something if you see it rather than hearing it. Similarly, your brand needs to stop talking about its qualities and features. Instead, your brand should focus on conveying the story about how it helped someone to fight their problem. This will have a greater impact. If you do so, your audience will be able to connect to the story and will see what difference your brand brought to that person's life, and this will make your audience trust you more. If you keep on boasting about how good your company is, it won't be of any help. You can choose any angle to connect to your audience. Sentiment and humor are the two most powerful angles when it comes to influencing people. When you go for the sentimental angle, it is very important for you to make the word selection carefully. You need to arrange your words and convey the story in such a manner that it plucks your audience's heartstrings.

- ***Don't Go for a Short Story:*** Always go for a long-term and ongoing story instead of a short one. Always remember that here you are trying to form an emotional bond with your client, so you want them to come back to you repeatedly. So, make sure that your story doesn't end in two lines. List down some of the struggles and challenges that the hero of your story will face but will finally overcome. It must be a continuing saga of events, difficulties, and achievements. People don't relate much to characters who are introduced to them for a brief moment, and then they face a small challenge that they overcome in a short time and then disappear. People face new problems each and every day. So, in order to make them relate to you, the hero of your story must face a huge trail of struggles too.

- *Be Consistent:* Do whatever it takes to maintain the values that you claim to have. In this internet age, people are very much well equipped to catch authentic people who are not what they claim to be. So, no matter what, never lose your consistency. If you violate your consumer's trust by not staying true to your story, you will be at a huge loss. Never contradict what your brand claims to have or offer. Your values should be a part of your brand story, so make them one. Don't forget to explain and elaborate as to why you follow them or how it will be beneficial to everyone. Don't change your message in different marketing campaigns. If you do so, you will lose authenticity. Be consistent with your thoughts, beliefs, vision, mission, values, and goals in each of your marketing campaigns.

- ***Let the Brand Story Focus on What Is Inside:*** Your origin story plays a huge role in making your brand story consistent and authentic. What made you start your business or from what you got the idea of doing what you do, constitute your origin story. Your origin story also comprises of the factors, other than money, that keep you motivated to work hard and give your best. If you convey an honest story of yourself struggling through the difficulties of starting a new business, it will definitely win people's hearts. It is a great way to personalize your brand.

- ***Grab People's Attention and Maintain It:*** It is very important to catch people's attention and make them invest their time and energy in you. You should know your audience first. You should know their driving factors, their likes, and dislikes, factors motivating them, etc. After knowing these things, base your story and the characters on their interests and preferences. Another effective way to grab people's attention is language. Business communication can be very effective in building a strong audience base if done correctly. You should be very careful with the tone you use while conveying your story. If you use the wrong tone, people will no longer stick to you.

Chapter 7: Step 7 - Market Your Brand

Marketing your brand is the most important thing that you must do for branding your business. Let us discuss some of the ways by which you will be able to successfully market your brand.

Create a Website

Though you have spent a lot of time perfecting your product, you should take another step ahead. When you are first starting out, it can be quite challenging to obtain the required market exposure. The best thing to do at this stage is to create meaningful contents that will help people to understand you, your brand, and what you will offer. By doing this, you will leave an impact on your potential customers so that when they will need something similar to what your offer, they will always be reminded of you. You will be able to generate prospective leads and will also entertain people. For turning your leads to sales, you need to focus on SEO.

SEO

When you are not a renowned brand, it is not possible for the people to know about your brand and the things you offer. You should focus on search engine optimization and find the keywords that your clients and customers will type in the search engine while searching for products or services similar to yours.

Use Social Media

Most of the world's population is active on social media on a regular basis. Instagram, Pinterest, Snapchat, Reddit, Twitter, and Facebook are the most popular ones. Don't try to master each and every one of them. Instead, try focusing on the aspects that set them apart from the rest and then choose the one that suits you the most. Once you have made your choice, start looking for ways to do social media marketing for your brand or company.

You Can Try Live Streaming

Different social media platforms allow their users to do live streaming. Facebook and YouTube are the most popular ones among them. By utilizing this facility, you will be able to build your audience base and convey your story to them.

Make Your Brand Unique

Due to the ocean of information around the web, people can say that no brand is unique anymore. But it is not always true. No person can copy you fully if you are charming, outrageous, or outspoken. These factors are responsible for making your brand unique.

Start Storytelling

The previous point goes hand-in-hand with this point. If you want your online audience to engage with you, and form an emotional connection with your brand, start getting personal. Share your story, which says about your vision, mission, goals, achievements, struggles, failures, and success. Only then will people be able to relate to you and form an emotional bond with you.

Try Influencer Marketing

It is a very well-known term now. Almost seventy-five percent of the brands use this particular marketing technique nowadays. You can also utilize social media posts, endorsements from experts or reliable brands, blogger reviews, etc. These will be fruitful only if you set realistic expectations through efficient storytelling.

Make Valuable Content

Great content is always loved by the customers. The same goes for Google as well. There are various ways by which you can share the services and products you offer, such as blogging, infographics, podcasts, videos, etc. This will increase leads and traffic and will also play a huge role in increasing your revenues. It will also make you appear as an authoritative expert on some given topic. In many cases, businessmen feel reluctant to create their own content. You are not alone in a situation like this.

There are many people like you, and they recruit freelance content creators, web designers, virtual assistants, and digital marketers to prepare top-notch content for their brands. Writers can also take your old content and give it a new spark. Make sure that you don't compromise with your content because your content is what people are going to judge you by. What you show or depict in your content is an integral part of business communication.

Publish on LinkedIn

We have already discussed the perks of social media marketing. LinkedIn is quite an efficient platform when it comes to establishing professional connections. LinkedIn was built as a professional tool for employers and employees. It has gained huge popularity in the last few years. This has just one meaning, i.e., the professionals use it as a platform to showcase their services, products, and values, which are well received by their audiences and thus making it a hit.

Help Others

If you provide your target audience some valuable information, it will contribute to building your brand awareness. One of the most well-used and influential tools to bring change is education. You can do this by conducting events, free classes, online webinars, podcasts, etc. Don't go easy on customers who have already purchased from you once. Efforts are always cherished. Treat your clients with the utmost sincere customer service for their satisfaction. Don't forget to keep a FAQ page on your website so that your audience can visit there and search for information related to their doubts; otherwise, they can end up going to your competitor brands.

Conduct Podcasts

Having their voices heard isn't a very pleasant idea for a lot of people out there. But you need to understand one thing clearly that thinking inside the box and procrastination is not going to take you anywhere. For marketing your brand, you have to think out of the box and be fearless and outspoken. If you are an owner who is proud of his brand that offers some product or service, then you need to maximize on podcasts. If your product or service is somewhat similar to products available in the market, it will be a little difficult to catch people's attention, but you should always try. It is better to try and fail rather than not trying at all.

Do Giveaways and Offer Discounts

Offering huge discounts can be a beneficial tool for attracting customers in the first place. You can do giveaways, i.e., send complimentary gifts. These make customers feel valued and incentivized. In simple words, make yourself ready to offer interesting complimentary gifts to your customers for the sake of building brand awareness and form connections with the customers. These are essential for reputation management. The gifts that you will give don't need to be very costly and extravagant; instead, minimalistic gifts like eBooks, etc., may be very attractive and lovely for your customers.

A few other examples of complementary gifts are small journals, key chains, pens, fridge magnets, etc. You can use social media for promoting your services and products along with the discounts and giveaways you are offering with it. In exchange for that, you can ask your customers to give genuine reviews on your site and thus building your company's goodwill. Don't forget that you will face a lot of challenges while trying to build your brand's awareness and while trying to form connections with people. Keep offering discounts and giveaways and keep promoting them regardless of the negativity.

Incorporate Infographics

Illustrations are a great way to catch people's eyes. If you display your market data in a bright and colorful way, then people are likely to take some time and observe it carefully. Since it offers credibility and faith, your customers will be much more dedicated to listening to this particular brand-building tool. Infographics that are easy to post, share, and read on social media are the finest contents that you should immediately start using.

Try Car Wraps

Car wraps are customized designs that cover your whole car and attracts plenty of attention to the message or business you want to promote. Leaving the mirrors and windows of your car, wrap the rest of your car and convert it into a giant moving advertisement. This is a very powerful way to attract people's eyes. You can either roam in it in your town or even park it in an event or a regular parking lot. Whatever you do, it is bound to attract people's eyes. In case you are short of budget to afford a company's car to try this, you can even try it on your own car. This will make people slowly get close and familiar with your brand.

Remarket Campaigns

Developing your brand's awareness is not that much effective without remarketing. You should not limit your ads to your own website. You should also place them all across the web in all the possible places. It is required to get maximum exposure. When your potential customers see your brand's advertisements everywhere, it will instigate a sense of trust and authority in them. Don't forget to maintain social media, podcasts, and blogs to make your customers realize how big of a brand yours is, even if it is not that big yet. Remarketing is a proven way to increase your conversion rates rapidly.

Try Paid Social Advertising

It is not easy to have an effective organic social marketing. This is because there are a lot of brands that are already out there and established. It is quite hard to beat them with the organic social marketing strategy. This is where paid social advertising kicks in. Twitter and Facebook are not that expensive compared to the level of exposure they offer. You should not be impatient. It will be very odd to expect results immediately after taking up paid social advertisements. Stay patient and keep doing what you do. Always remember that every single step towards familiarity and publicity will take you one step closer to your desired goals.

Networking

Conducting networking events such as trade shows, company parties are a great way to build brand awareness. It will give you a time out from your regular office schedule and will also let you meet many people who can turn out to be a potential client or a customer in the future. Don't go with a mentality of just selling your products and services. Instead, go with an open mind that is always ready to educate itself, know about other people's struggles and success stories. This will help you to connect with people on a genuine and personal level.

Conclusion

Thank you for making it through to the end of *Business Branding*, let's hope it was informative and able to provide you with all of the tools you need to achieve your goals, whatever they may be.

The next step is to start applying these steps to your business one by one. There are many areas to develop when it comes to branding your business, and you should not overlook things like customer service and reputation management.

But start with the basic ones and then work your way up the ladder. Don't rush the process because it is this process of branding that will determine how your customers see you as a brand and whether the profile that you have created is grabbing the right attention or not.

Once you have put your time and effort into creating a new brand, you should have no problem attracting customers. All that is left for you to do, after you have created your brand, is engage in efficient marketing and advertising.

Book 2: Social Media Marketing

7 Easy Steps to Master Social Media Advertising, Influencer Marketing & Platform Audience Growth

Santino Spencer

Introduction

Welcome to *Social Media Marketing;* whether you are trying to run a business or just up your social media marketing game, you have made a great choice. The seven steps shared within *Social Media Marketing* will provide great value to enhance your success. Every business, regardless of size, has to have some type of strategy for social media marketing. Simply going about social media marking without a plan can be very costly and honestly might even hurt your brand.

Social media has become the fastest moving industry in the world. Businesses can grow faster, find new customers quicker, grow their wealth and knowledge by reaching out to people from all over the world. This is something that was not possible several decades ago when the only form of marketing accessible to most businesses was print, radio, and television advertising. Your reach was restricted based on your budget, and you had no control over how many times your target audience would listen or see the content you are putting out there. Well, not anymore.

One of social media's most powerful features is the way it can connect people from all over the world in a matter of seconds. It doesn't matter where you are located, as long as you have a working internet connection and some device to view content on, you're connected. For businesses, this has been an *incredible* advantage. Imagine the business potential when you can now reach millions of customers worldwide?

Social media has changed the world of marketing forever. For example, your business can go live in a matter of seconds to people across the world. Your product launch, when it is done as live broadcast, it is instantly shown to customers from every country imaginable. You get to share the amazing things that happen in your company with your loyal customers and build relationships with them in a way that you never could before social media came along.

This platform has forced businesses to become more creative, innovative, and more attentive to what the customers want in order to keep the content fresh, relevant, and appealing to the target audience. Social media has also become a hotbed of research, and this is where *your business* begins to transform your marketing strategies. The seven-step approach in the next few chapters will be your guide to marketing your business on this social, digital space like a winner. Let's get started.

Chapter 1: Step 1 – Understand Why Your Business Needs It

Social media is the king of the marketing world. There is no one out there who *has not* heard of social media and what an incredible force it can be. Companies have gone from being unknown to a household name through the sheer power of social media marketing alone. Since it was created, social media has changed and revolutionized the internet. Despite the pros and cons, there is no denying that every single business out there is going to need social media marketing to remain competitive.

More importantly, you need social media if you want to stay in business. Customers these days *expect* you to have some kind of social media presence before they can even think about taking you seriously. Let's put it this way, if your competitor has a social media presence and you don't, they are going to go to your competitors, no matter how fabulous your product may be.

What Is It?

Customers don't want to be handed flyers or brochures with your sales pitch on it anymore. Customers today are only going to be interested in what you have to sell if you find a way to engage with them in an interesting and relevant way. That is where social media comes into play. Social media marketing is basically marketing that is done on social media platforms. You will be using platforms like Facebook, Instagram, or Twitter, for example, to announce new product launches, introduce new services, talk about your latest line, and a whole lot more. Yes, it is that simple.

To be honest, it is not that far different from the old marketing methods that businesses and companies have been employing even before social media was a thing. It is still marketing, except this time, all the tools and techniques of marketing have been modified to accommodate social media platforms. You're marketing your products on social media instead of print, television, and radio this time.

Social media marketing is an approach that businesses can utilize to interact with their customers and potential customers in the most natural way possible. This can easily be done on the bigger, more popular platforms like Facebook and Twitter, and it can also be done on smaller niche sites that are built around communities. Think of social media as a town hall, where every customer comes together to share stories, ideas, thoughts, opinions, and feedback about a product or service. To touch base with new prospective customers that may be coming through your pipeline and convert them into loyal, paying customers, you need social media platforms to help you achieve that goal.

As for your customers, social media platforms are not marketing machines but social networks. When you start embarking on developing your social media marketing strategy, you may be up against a few challenges. Plenty of companies to in hard and start hard selling to their consumers, which inundates their followers with discount offer codes and new product announcement, even before consumers could even warm up to the brand. When their accounts do not bring the traffic they want, these brands assume that these networks aren't a good fit for them or social media isn't the place to spend their efforts on.

Why Your Business Needs It

There are several reasons why your business needs social media marketing, and these are some of the reasons why you should be utilizing this form of communication as soon as possible:

- *Your Marketing Costs Go Down* - This is probably one of the things businesses love most about social media platforms is the ability to reduce their marketing cost. Yes, it is going to reduce your marketing costs by *a lot*. Compared to traditional marketing methods like print advertising, television, billboards, magazines, or radio channels, marketing on social media is remarkably more affordable.

Don't forget that social media channels itself are *free,* and it does not cost anything to create a free social media account for your business to get the ball rolling.

- *It Is the Best Way to Showcase Your Brand* - Social media marketing is by far the best way to showcase your brand these days. In fact, it has become the number one way for a business to increase its brand recognition without having to spend a ton of money on traditional advertising methods. Social media marketing gives your business the opportunity to boost your reputation through your website, search engine optimization, email marketing, and more.

  It is an opportunity to drive sales and build relationships with your customers by interacting with them on a one-to-one level, something that was not possible before with traditional forms of marketing. What is even better is that you get to communicate with your customers through your social media pages for *free.* It costs you nothing to respond to their comments, chat messages, and queries. Each time you do that, you're building a connection with your customers, and in the business world, this form of communication and interaction is priceless.

- *You're Developing a Loyal Following and Community* - By creating these relationships with your customers, you are indirectly building a loyal community among them as you do this. People have always enjoyed being a part of something. People enjoy being part of a group, a crowd, a club, something that makes them feel a sense of belonging and acceptance. Today, businesses have the opportunity to create such a community among the people through social media marketing. Your customers will enjoy being associated with a brand that is actively building a lively community online, especially if they get to interact with other like-minded customers for some honest feedback and opinions about your products and services.

Customers want value for money these days, and reviews online alone are not going to cut it. They want recommendations and suggestions straight from the horse's mouth, and in this case, the proverbial horse would be the other customers. By building a community like this, you are helping your customers establish an emotional connection with your brand, and if you trigger the right emotions, you make them customers for life. This is the kind of relationship that is essential for your long-term success.

- ***Better Customer Service*** - A successful business is no longer about just the purchase and sale of products anymore. Customers expect more than merely purchasing your products and letting that be the end of the story. Oh no, these days, customers want to share their feedback and thoughts about your products, and social media is the best channel for them to do this. Not only does social media allow your customers to communicate directly with your company, but they can also communicate with each other. Word of mouth is one of the best forms of free marketing you can get your hands on.

There is nothing like a good word or recommendation from a source to have other customers flocking to your business, eager to get their hands on your products too. Plus, being able to communicate directly with your business helps to enhance your brand's trustworthiness while simultaneously improving your customer service. With the old way of marketing, a business was nothing more than a cold, distant entity to the customer. Today, businesses and customers can interact instantaneously with each other as old friends would.

- *It Increases Your Digital Exposure* - By actively interacting on your social media channels, you are significantly increasing your online presence. A customer will remember and prefer a business that is actively responding to their messages or comments within a reasonable timeframe. One of the reasons why social media is an incredible platform for maximizing your brand's exposure is because of its worldwide presence. It is accessible to everyone in the world with an internet connection and at least a smartphone.

Social media accounts are free to set up, and this means that every single one of your customers is ninety-nine percent very likely to own at least one type of social media account. In fact, a lot of shopping these days happens on social media accounts, not just websites alone anymore. The massive number of daily users and its incredible content-sharing capabilities means news about your business will spread in a matter of seconds. Five minutes from now, your brand name could be introduced to someone halfway across the world from you, all through the incredible power of social media.

- *It Helps to Boost Your Traffic and Search Engine Rating* - Social media platforms are major lead generators. They bring a consistent stream of high-volume traffic to your website and maximize your search engine optimization (SEO). Search engines can significantly reflect your social media content with the right keywords. This is potential that no business can afford to miss out on.

- *It Expands Your Sales and Reaches New Groups of Audiences Quickly* - Nothing else can generate new sales and reach new customers as quickly as social media can, once again, thanks to its incredible worldwide reach. By monitoring and listening to the conversations that are happening on your social media pages *from your customers,* this is an opportunity to address their needs *specifically.* Businesses never had this opportunity before social media came along. Back then, you could only guess the specifics of what your customer wanted based on surveys or questionnaires. By addressing what they need, it expands your sales and increases your customer base.

Traditional forms of marketing, while still being used today, are slowly on their way out. It is the age of the internet where everything is online, everything is immediate, and almost everyone is accessible with just a few clicks of the mouse. Social media platforms are the easiest and most convenient way for people to keep in touch even if they may be halfway across the globe. Businesses realize that today's consumer is shifting away from those old advertising forms. Today, the attention is on social media platforms, and this is where you need to be. You need to go where your customers are.

Chapter 2: Step 2 - Market Research Done Right

Did you know that social media marketing could be used for in-depth information into your market research process? For any business, it is important that your product or service is all about the consumer. Everything that you do should be all about your customers. This is where market research plays a vital role in keeping up with what your customers want and expect from your business. Since they are paying money for your products and services, they will be expecting you to provide what they are looking for.

What Is Social Media Market Research?

This is the type of research that acknowledges your branding and the way that your business is reaching your target audience. In other words, it tells you whether your marketing campaigns are effectively progressing the way that you hoped it would. It gives you insight into the marketing methods you have been using on each of your social media platforms in the past, present, and future. The research conducted will point out whether your efforts have been effective in achieving your business goals.

The Benefits of Market Research

For the answers to your *who, what, where, when, why*, and *how* questions, you need market research. Market research is a valuable tool that has long been used by businesses to better understand the needs and demands of their target audience base. Thanks to social media, however, not only do businesses get to research what their customers are up to, they also get to research what their competitors are doing too. The kiss of death for any business is to assume that they know that the customers' needs are, or to assume that they should just go ahead and build a business first, and the marketing will take care of bringing the customers in. That is just a warrant for failure.

In the business world, every single decision that is being made in the interest of the business needs to have a foundation on concrete and undeniable research proof behind it, even for campaigns that are being run on social media. Besides giving you intel into the minds of your customers, market research is beneficial for the following reasons:

- It keeps you focused on your business plan and ensures that you are always looking ahead at what the next step should be.

- It reminds you to listen to your target audience whenever you're thinking about coming up with a new product or service line. Give the people what they want, and they will keep coming back to you for more.

- It tells you what problems you need to solve for your customers and helps you create the right product to get the job done.

- Market research helps you identify what your business opportunities are. When you know what the customer wants, you can start strategizing about what needs to be done to meet those needs and demands. This puts you in a unique position to take advantage of opportunities your competition may not have had a chance to yet.

- Market research ensures that you stay relevant, and in doing so, you keep your business relevant. Staying relevant and keeping your customers loyal is about being able to meet and fulfill the needs that they have. If they don't get it from your business, they will get it from your competitors, and there is no amount of marketing you can do that will keep your customers with you if you are not meeting their needs.

- It cuts down on the risks and losses you experience per campaign. Research supplies your business with the necessary and vital information you need to decide on what the right approach or the next step should be. This keeps the risks to a minimum because you will not be stumbling blindly forward hoping that their plan is going to work. With your research in hand, you will know for a fact what the right move should be because they have the research on hand to back it up.

- Market research helps to point out what your current and potential business issues are. As a business, you need to pay close attention to the feedback that is being received by your market research audience because oftentimes, they will be able to shed light on an area that may not even be seen as a problem for the company but raises issues with its target market.

- Market research makes your customers feel happy because it tells them that your business is listening to their concerns. When customers feel that they are being heard and that a business is taking the time to find out what they want, there is a higher chance that they will remain loyal to the businesses.

Primary and Secondary Market Research

Market research is divided into two categories, primary and secondary. Primary market research is the most important type of research for your business. It is research that is done in real-time, and it is research that you are doing yourself. Primary research is where you start from scratch with information that does not exist yet. Not until you create it. You are conducting this research to find the information and data that you need. Traditionally, primary market research was a costly affair. It was conducted through focus groups, interviews, and surveys. In this aspect, social media has been a complete game-changer. With social media, the valuable primary market research information you need can be collected *for free.* You can conduct polls on social media for free, conduct interviews with special guests on your live streams and make a note of the questions your customers ask, and much more.

Your secondary research is information that already exists, like your customers' interests based on their profiles, the types of questions they've already asked you. All you have to do is analyze the existing research to see how you can use it to your advantage. Examples of where you would go for secondary research include case studies conducted by your competitors if the information is available online, tuning in to your competitor's live streams, or analyzing the results from previous campaigns and surveys you have conducted in the past.

Both primary and secondary research have their benefits, but primary research has a more personalized factor to it. Plus, primary research gives you access to the latest information that is relevant to your customers. Today, you can run polls on your Facebook and Instagram stories. It only takes mere seconds for your customers to quickly tap on the answers they prefer, and there you go. You have instant answers to your questions. The authenticity of the information you gather from this approach is extraordinary. For example, by showcasing different products across your Instagram or Facebook

Stories feature throughout the week, you might be surprised to learn which are your most popular and least popular products. With access to information like this, you can instantly revise your key selling points and campaign focus as you go.

Social Media Channels That Are Good for Research

The different social media channels can provide insight and contribute to your research in various ways:

- *Facebook Groups* - Join a Facebook group that your target audience is part of and start participating in the discussions. If you prefer to be a passive observer that just watches and reads what people are talking about in these groups, you can do that too. Facebook Groups also give you the option of using question polls as part of your research. You can type out a question (a primary market research method) and get the answers that you are looking for to help you develop your next content or product.

- *Twitter* - Twitter allows you the option of creating lists. You can put your target audience on these lists, either on one list or a couple of different lists, depending on what your research objective is. Having these lists makes it easier for you to scroll through to find out what your customer interests are, what content they are tweeting about, the hashtags they use, and more. You also have the option of creating a competitor's list, where you put your competitors on a specific list to go through to research the type of content they are putting out, the hashtags they use, and the content they are tweeting about too.

- *YouTube* - On YouTube, you can source for content that is similar to yours and go through the comments section to see the types of questions that are being asked. You can find out a surprising amount of information about your target audience this way, like the types of problems they have and the answers they are looking for. By going through these comments, it can help you develop content that *they* are interested in, enticing them to your page instead of your competitor's.

- *Live Streams* - These Live Streams are available on most social media platforms. It notifies your followers when your business is broadcasting live. For example, once you start your live stream, your customers that follow your account are going to get a notification on their phone saying you've gone live, and they'll quickly tune in to your content. This is a fantastic approach to conducting some immediate market research by conducting a question and answer session.

- *Surveys* - This one is a traditional marketing tactic that has existed even before the days of the internet. Surveys are a primary market research method that is still being used today because it still has a purpose. Websites like Survey Monkey make it easy to quickly create a free survey that you can quickly send to your customers. You can post your survey on your Facebook page, website, Instagram, and other social media platforms that you prefer.

Chapter 3: Step 3 - How to Market on Facebook

You could be just starting out with your Facebook marketing tactics, or you could be a seasoned marketer. Either way, every business is always on the lookout for ways to improve their marketing strategies so they can market on Facebook like a winner. Whether your goal is to boost your following or engagement rate, no matter what your goals are, you need to have the right strategies in order to make it work. Facebook is a crowded space with millions of contents being shared daily by individual users and businesses alike. The only way to be a winner in this platform is to stand out with the right marketing tactics.

Your Content Is Where the Magic Happens

Facebook is your platform, but your content is where the magic happens. If you want your content to stand out, it has to be incredible. There is a lot of content that gets posted on Facebook daily, and this means it is going to take something remarkable to make an impression on your target audience. Your content is not the only one they will be exposed to on a daily basis, and it is important that you make a strong enough first impression with every piece of content you post if you want your business to stay at the forefront of their minds.

As businesses, brands, and marketers, quality content should be your focal point with everything that you post. Before you hit the publish button, the question you need to ask yourself is, *"is my content worth noticing?"*. A good tip to keep in mind when you are trying to create and curate your quality content is to focus on a niche. Instead of trying to target the billions of users on Facebook, even though it is tempting to try and bring in as many customers as possible, you will be much better off targeting a subset of users instead. This makes it much easier to produce useful content that is equally entertaining to this niche group. When you know who you are targeting and what they want to see from you, it makes it easier to come up with quality content that matters.

Another way to create quality content is to focus on what your goals are. For example, if your goal was to drive traffic to your website, then you would focus on content that is specifically designed to encourage your target audience to flock to your website. Having goals in mind gives you a purpose, and with that purpose, you can begin creating the type of content you need to meet those goals. For effective marketing, ninety percent of your time should be spent on creating content, while the other ten percent of that time is focused on posting the content. Avoid the mistake of getting too caught up with trying to post as much as possible in the hopes of staying relevant on your audience's page. They would much rather see you post once a day but posting something that is useful to them, instead of posting frivolous content five times a day. It is not the quantity; it is the quality that matters.

Focus on Creating Video Content

The majority of your audience these days is going to be more interested in video content over everything else. Mark Zuckerberg himself once said that videos are the future of social media. Facebook's algorithm even focuses on placing video content at the top of the newsfeed. If you were to analyze your statistics over the course of a few months, you would probably notice that your video content is going to see the most successful compared to any other type of content you produce. You don't need a lot of resources or a big team to create quality video content. In fact, it is much easier than you think, and quality content begins by keeping these few tips in mind when you're making your videos:

- Avoid being too "sales-y" with your videos. Videos should be used as a brand awareness tool, not a sales pitch.

- Keep your videos to a maximum of two minutes. The top-performing videos on this platform are usually between sixty and ninety seconds long.

- Keep the captions in your videos between fifty to a hundred characters. Your audience does not have time to read long and lengthy captions. Ideally, you want your captions to capture the gist of the overall message.

Another important factor to keep in mind is that more than ninety percent of your audience is most likely going to be viewing your content on their mobile phones. This means that your target audience would be scrolling through their feed quickly, and therefore, they don't have time for long and lengthy content. Users have very short attention spans, and they will easily be distracted by other things going on around them. To win them over, you need to keep your videos short, to the point, and put your *best content* at the *front of your video.* You only have seconds to intrigue your audience enough to make them watch your video all the way through, and you need to make those first few seconds count.

Why You Should Be Sharing Curated Content

Creating new content is time-consuming, and despite your best efforts, there may be times when you are so busy running the business that you simply don't have time to create new content. To supplement this, what you could do is share curated content. Share content from another top, reputable source that is from within your industry. You don't have to worry about replacing the content strategy of your own business when you do this. Sharing curated content is merely a supplement to help you maintain a consistent voice and posting on social media.

There is a benefit to sharing curated content from other sources too. If all you do is post content about your business all the time, people are going to start tuning you out after a while because it is all the same thing. There is nothing that keeps it fresh, interesting, and exciting on your page. By sharing curated content from others, you are strengthening your position as an industry leader, showing your audience your vast knowledge on the subject. Another benefit of doing this is that you get to build relationships with the people whose content you are sharing.

Repurpose Your Top Performing Content

Do you have content that has performed well in the past? Why not share it again? Not all your users are going to see every piece of content that you post. There is no harm in re-sharing old content. The one rule of thumb to keep in mind when you do this is to wait at least a month before you re-share any piece of content. Allow some time to pass before you put this post up again. Ideally, you would want a never-ending supply of fresh, new, and great content you can post to your Facebook page. However, since this is not always the case, your next best option would be to re-share what already proved to be popular in the past.

Focus on Your "Pages to Watch"

This is one of the most powerful tools you can use to create great social media content. You will get access to your "Pages to Watch" feature once you have seventy-five likes or more on your page. With this feature, you get to watch up to a hundred pages. It could be your competitors, inspirational pages that you love, and any sort of page you would like. Once you have a list of pages that you can find inspiration from daily, you can use this for ideas to guide your own Facebook strategy. The top three ways to use this "Pages to Watch" feature include the following:

- You could use this as a guide to set goals and benchmarks for your own brand. For example, you could use it to set audience engagement or growth goals.

- You could use this feature to curate content. Facebook even ranks the most popular type of content first, literally making your job easier by telling you what content has proven to be the most popular on other similar pages.

Listen to Your People

A lot of businesses will say that they struggle to come up with content. Why do they struggle? Because they are not listening to their audience. One of the most important foundations of any marketing strategy, whether it is social media or conventional marketing techniques, is listening to your target market. If you listen to your people, they will *tell you what they want to see and hear from you.* You don't have to spend hours brainstorming new and fresh ideas, all you have to do is learn to listen. Once you have gathered these details, you can create content that is tailored to their interests and needs and spark conversations that lead to sales.

Chapter 4: Step 4 - How to Market on Instagram

If you want your Instagram following to grow, it is important to have a strategy that works. This rule of thumb can be applied to all your social media platforms, truth be told. Instagram is a platform that is focused heavily on visual content. It is less about the captions and more about the captivating images. Just like Facebook, this platform is also one of the stronger social media tools for marketing and brand building, although it uses a different approach. Instagram's core strengths lie in its vivid imagery gallery, and for businesses like retailers, clothing companies, jewelry companies, travel companies, and any business that relies heavily on presenting itself through images, this is an excellent social media platform to do so. Instagram should be treated as a marketing tool and part of your entire overall marketing strategy. It may be a powerful social media platform, but it is not a standalone method for building your business.

Instagram has the potential to generate hundreds of new customers each month, but only if you're going about it the right way.

You Need to Have a Plan

You need to have a plan because it is going to guide your efforts and point you in the right direction. Your outcome is going to be a lot more fruitful if you have a good sense of where you should be going.

When you are developing your marketing strategy, spend some time thinking about what your primary goal with your Instagram account is. Avoid simply snapping and recording anything just for the sake of appearing active on your social media account. In order to post successfully captivating images and videos, the content needs to tell a story. All images and videos that get posted on Instagram will be a reflection of your business, and therefore, you want each content you put out there to link back to your overall business goals.

Here's a hint you might not have thought about. Your goal *should not be* trying to grow your following. That's right, you need to think bigger than that. Your goals should be along the lines of getting more traffic to your website, building your email list, boosting the sales of your products or service, and not about how many likes you can get on a picture you posted this morning or how many followers you've gained. Of course, it is always good news to see your numbers growing in terms of followers. It means your business is getting noticed, but there is a lot more potential to be tapped into with Instagram. Think bigger with your goals and use Instagram to help you reach those goals.

Create Shareable Content

What most businesses would do is create content that is focused entirely on their business. Of course, that is what you should be doing, isn't it? Are you only creating content that is all about you? Well, not necessarily. What you should do instead is create content that other people can share.

Identify Who Your Target Market Is

Not sure who your target market is? Then you have work to do. Like all social media platforms, you need to know who your target market is because it is an important element of your business. Your customers are the lifeline of your business, and if you target the wrong groups, you're wasting all the time, energy, and resources you committed to marketing on Instagram. Since Instagram can be a rather time-consuming platform, you want to make sure that everything you do on this platform has a purpose.

Since Instagram is limited to visual postings, you need to think about how to take your connection with your followers a step further by reaching out even more. One example of how you do this is to provide a link in your description section that directs back to your company's website or landing page. A lot of websites these days have a call to action feature the minute a user lands on their site by either asking them to simply subscribe to a newsletter.

This is why it is important to identify your target market. When a user subscribes, companies get access to the user's email, and this will then allow them to send updates and reach out to the users directly into their inbox. When posting images and videos on your social media platform, prompt the audience with a call to action by redirecting them back to the link on your bio. Your target market will be the group of people who will benefit the most from your offerings. This is going to be different for every business, depending on what your brand and your business represent. Identify as much information as you can about your target market, and this will allow you to create content that is specifically relevant to what they want to see from you.

Your Account Needs to Be Visible

Avoid the mistake of making your account private. You would be surprised at how often this little detail gets overlooked. Privatizing your personal account is fine, but your business account should remain as accessible as possible. Your target customers and audience base need to be able to locate you on Instagram, and it won't help if your account is private, and they have no access to the content your business offers unless they follow your account. Your target customers don't want to feel like they are being forced into joining or following your business, they want to be able to choose it. Make your content visible and easy to find on the social media platform, and make it likable enough that the audience wants to keep tabs with what you're doing by being a follower.

Use Your Hashtags Sparingly

Hashtags are the most popular on Instagram, although Twitter and Facebook do incorporate the use of hashtags on their platforms as well, it was never still quite as popular as it is on Instagram. In fact, one of the primary ways of discovering a new person, product, group, or business on Instagram is through hashtags. Hashtags are one of Instagram's main marketing strengths because not only does it make it easy for users to discover a business, businesses also find it easier to track potential consumers. Avoid being tempted to bombard your post with every single hashtag that pops into your mind. Focus on the ones that link back to your business.

Customers and audiences who are on the lookout for something specific will have a better chance of locating your content when the right hashtags have been put into place. The key tip here is to ensure everything posted, from content to texts and hashtags are in unison and complement one another. Before posting any content, it's recommended that you look at the trending hashtags of the day and narrow down the ones that are related to your business and content. If it's relevant then go ahead and use it, but if it's not, then ditch it.

Create Content That Is Strategic

Once you deeply understand who your target audience is, creating content that matters becomes a whole lot easier. Every photo, video, and the caption that you take should speak directly to your customer.

Be clear about what your business is offering. Your content should offer a solution and provide value to your customers and your followers. If your target customers and the audience are not sure of what your business is selling, you lose the potential to gain new customers because they will lose interest.

People like to know what they're dealing with, and businesses who don't have a strong, clear presence and message are going to be on the losing end. When you aim to create content specifically for a demographic, you are going to naturally attract them to your Instagram feed. They will decide that they *want* to follow you because they can relate to everything that you post. When your content makes them feel like you are speaking directly to them, it can convert them into loyal, paying customers. If you create random content, you might end up attracting a mix of people and get a higher number of followers, but they might not take the action that you want.

Engage with Your Target Audience Regularly

To consistently attract the right kind of audience who will take the action you want, you need to engage with your target market regularly.

Create Vertical Video Content

Video marketing is a must for anyone running a business. Many successful businesses acknowledge that videos are crucial and a necessary tool as part of their overall marketing strategy. To make the best impact possible on your viewers, you need to fully utilize the video marketing capabilities on Instagram. Thanks to videos being primarily shot on smartphones these days by users themselves, the vertical video trend has increased in popularity so much that they outperform the horizontal videos in every way.

It's a mobile world out there. Users are on their mobiles more than their desktops these days. At the end of each video, don't forget to include a call to action that will ask and remind your audience to take a specific action. A call to action encourages your audience to take the next step toward your primary goal and move along in your marketing funnel.

Chapter 5: Step 5 - How to Market on YouTube

What videos should you make for your business's YouTube channel? How will your target audience find you? Where do you even begin making content that is going to get your business noticed and skyrocket your marketing goals? It all comes down to three key things:

- Your strategy
- How to set up your channel
- How to secure your first few subscribers

Your YouTube Marketing Strategy

YouTube is one of the best platforms for business to engage with current and prospective customers because not only is YouTube a cost-effective marketing platform, but it has a much bigger reach than any other video dissemination platform out there. With more than a billion users to date and counting, this is one marketing opportunity you cannot afford to pass up.

YouTube is such an easy marketing tool for businesses to make use of because of how easy it is to share videos online. YouTube videos are also easily shareable on other social media platforms, which makes it easy for businesses to promote the content many times

100

over on their other social media accounts like Facebook and Twitter, doubling or tripling a YouTube video's reach just like that.

Now, the number one mistake that a lot of companies make with YouTube is not creating content *and thumbnails* that are interesting enough. Yes, your thumbnails have to be equally attractive because that is the first thing your customers will look at. Would you click on a thumbnail that didn't intrigue you? Probably not, and your customers will think the same. Many businesses get so caught up in creating interesting content of value that they forget they need to make their thumbnails attractive on their profile too.

The first step in creating a marketing strategy on YouTube is just like any other social platform, and it begins with defining your goals. With YouTube, you want to write down specific targets that you want to achieve, such as clicks and traffic, engagement as well as reach and subscriber numbers. If you want your audience to watch your videos, then you need to make videos that they *want to watch*. Otherwise, they are not going to watch, it is as simple as that.

The questions to ask when you're thinking about crafting your YouTube strategy for your video content are:

- What value can I add to my videos that the customer would appreciate?
- What is my target audience interested in?

- What videos would my target audience be willing to watch willingly without them feeling like they are being forced into it?

Value is added to your videos by *teaching* your audience something new, something useful, and something that will benefit them. You also add value by entertaining them through your videos and triggering emotions. How-to videos are among the high-performing videos on YouTube because they provide plenty of value to users. Since YouTube is the second most used search engine, people go to YouTube because they want to see something done or learn how to make something or cook something or build something.

How-To videos are great for plenty of business, no matter what industry you are in. If you are using this format, you need to look at what aspect of your business can be turned into a "How-To." For instance, you sell car engine oil. You can do a tutorial on how to use this oil, how to change your car engine oil, and the benefits of good oil. Look upon the internet for blog posts for materials you can use to create your video. Make this video edutainment.

Setting Up Your Channel

There are two types of channels you can set up. The first type of channel is where you have your profile as your main channel. The second channel is your brand channel. You need to set up a brand channel to gain access to the features you need to share with your employees and other people in the company who are also working on maintaining your channel. Every channel needs to have the following design elements:

- Your profile picture
- Your channel image
- Custom thumbnails (remember, your thumbnails need to be just as interesting and engaging as your videos)

An important note to keep in mind is that you need the elements on your channel to be consistent. Your brand needs to be represented in all your content. There are several ways you can optimize your channel too, and some of these elements are within your control, and some are not. Keywords that you use and how you use them are completely in your control, however, elements like how many people subscribe immediately after viewing your videos are not exactly things that you can control or have power on.

Going back to the importance of thumbnails, the right kind of thumbnail will attract a reader to click on it, making your video trend as well as make your channel recognizable. Just like the title, your thumbnail should be relevant to the content as well as correspond with your video title. Attractive thumbnails result in higher clicks. You should also include short descriptions in your thumbnail so viewers can understand what your video is all about. You want to immediately catch the interest of your viewers by telling them a quick story just by your thumbnails and your title. Not only should these elements tell viewers what your video is all about, but it should also make them curious enough to want to watch your videos. Make a template or style guide for your thumbnails to maintain consistency here too.

Getting Your First Few Subscribers

Getting your first few subscribers is usually one of the biggest challenges that a company would face on YouTube. In such a vast space with millions of videos all vying for your attention, how do you get your content to stand out enough that people *want* to subscribe to your channel? This is even more important if you're already a big and established brand since it can look rather unprofessional if you only have a few subscribers. Well, the first step is easy, and that is to leverage your existing social media accounts. Use your Facebook, Twitter, Instagram, newsletters, and blogs to get the ball rolling. Try to send the existing audience there over to your channel.

Another thing that you could do is to work together with other channels and other YouTubers. Video collaboration is popular among YouTubers, and it is a great way to gain a new audience base as well as increase your subscriber base. It is a win-win situation for both YouTubers as well as the target audience since the audience will get to see their favorite YouTubers together working on something or creating something. Working with influencers is not an uncommon strategy. In fact, many brands are starting to leverage the potential that working with influencers can bring to their business. Collaboration has so many obvious advantages, so long as you do it with the right people and brands.

Social media influencers are powerful. They can drive traffic to your Facebook page overnight by simply putting in a few good words and a well-crafted video upload. Especially if they're demonstrating how your product is being used. According to Forbes, what they revealed was that MuseFind, an influencer marketing platform, found that audiences were ninety-two percent more likely to trust the word of a social media influencer compared with an ad. Sometimes, these brands or people don't necessarily have to be in your industry, and you could try looking for complimenting brands and influencers to work with as this will grow your audience exponentially. The potential for content creation here is enormous.

Collaboration is one of the very best ways to add some entertainment value to your content. Apart from connecting with your audience, you can also use social media to connect with experts, influencers, and industry leaders, thus enhancing your status as an authoritative expert and credible source of information for your industry. The huge rise of social media platforms has also given birth to a new trend of social media influencers. These influencers use their popularity to market products and services to generate income.

An influencer is an individual who has huge popularity or followers that listen or emulate them. They collaborate with marketers to promote products, services, and even events to their followers. This has pushed many ad agencies to increase their budget on social media influencer marketing to catch this trend. A social media influencer is described as someone who has a lot of followers online. They are generally an expert or an authority on a particular subject, although celebrities fall under the influencer category too because of the immense pull they have. What an influencer buys, wears, or says can influence the decision of their followers. Over time, you are more than just a brand, you are part of a community. This change of perception also leads towards higher ROI, which means you'll also get plenty of exposure. With higher ROI, you get more exposure, and with more exposure, comes leads and new leads turn into followers. These followers turn into potential customers.

Chapter 6: Step 6 - Focusing on the Right Niche Market

Everyday there are thousands of people are searching for various products and services to buy. They might need these products and services to help fulfil a need or want that they have. Your job as a business is to find the right people who are looking for the kind of products and services that you offer. Those specific people are your niche market group.

What Is a Niche Market?

A niche market is a group of people who are looking for a specific product. For example, if your business was selling health supplements, your niche market would be that specific group of people who were looking for the kind of health supplements you provide. Your niche market would depend on the kind of products and services that you sell. Another example would be if you were in the business of selling baby products. Baby products can be divided into a few categories, like baby shoes, clothing, food, bath products, and more. Baby shoes would be one of the niche market consumers you would target.

If you want to grow your business and achieve all your goal milestones, then you need to be focused on marketing to your niche audience. The logic behind this is simple, if your audience is far too broad and general, a lot of your efforts could be wasted on targeting those who are not even remotely interested in your content. The narrower and more niche your target audience is, the better your return on investment will be. This will help you write better content, more compelling posts, and more engaging information. These benefits, however, extend beyond marketing. You create brand loyalty and credibility, it helps you identify customer pain points, create a loyal following, refine product strategies, and improve sales conversions. To be effective with your marketing strategy, you need to aim for where it matters the most. This strategy will end up saving you a lot of time, money, and effort in the long run.

How Do You Find Your Niche Market?

It would depend once again on the kind of products or services you sell. The first thing you need to do is to find a focus. Niche marketing is all about focus. It is a focus on selling and advertising your strategies towards a targeted portion of the market. You do not market to everyone who could benefit from your product or service. Instead, you niche market your products to specific people, focusing exclusively on a group of people or a demographic section of likely customers that would most definitely enjoy or benefit from your products. If you are a writer, you could narrow your focus by limiting your writing to children's books. From there, you can narrow your focus even further by focusing only on books for little girls. You could get even more specific by defining the age range you want to target. The more specific you get with your targeting, the more niche your target market becomes.

You could target your audience based on geographic area, lifestyle, occasion, profession, style, culture, activity or habits, behavior, demographic, need, and more. The biggest concern that businesses have when it comes to niche marketing is the fear of losing out on thousands of potential customers. By narrowing your focus like that, you might be concerned that other people are missing out on your products, and therefore, you are missing out on a potential sale. This is a catch twenty-two because the answer is both yes and no. Not every business can be as booming as Amazon is, selling products that cater to practically everyone on the planet. Even if you do want to be like Amazon, Amazon didn't start out that way in the beginning. They had a specific niche they were focusing on too, and they sold books. Over time, they eventually progressed to the Amazon that we know and love today, where they are selling products in almost every category.

When you define a niche for yourself, you enter into a market with potentially less competition. Niche marketing's biggest benefit would be that it allows brands to stand out from the pack and appear unique. This will make sure it resonates better with its already unique and distinct customer section. A brand can employ niche marketing initiatives to stand out and be more valuable rather than blend in, to reach a higher growth potential and ultimately build a better, stronger, and long-lasting relationship with its target market. When you have a shoestring budget, or you're just getting started in the business world, minimal competition is good news, and that is why you should start out by focusing on a niche.

How do you determine what is the best niche market for your business? Through a lot of research, for one thing. There is going to be a lot of research that is going to go into this stage of your business, but it has to be done. You need to research, compare, and evaluate the current market trends and what you have to work with. When researching prices of items for example, look at several platforms instead of focusing on just one. For example, research current trends on Amazon and eBay, but don't make those the only platforms that you are looking at. Broaden your search to include different types of niches. Look at the higher-priced bracket items, and compare that to the lower bracket items. Compare and evaluate the market trends that you are observing on this platform. What is selling well and what isn't. What trends seem to be doing well and why? The more areas of your business that your research covers, the better.

Finding the right niche is also much easier when you aim to answer the following questions. More importantly, this framework is going to help you find a *profitable niche.* These questions are something that every business can use as a framework to find their target audience. The questions to ask as you seek to pinpoint your niche market include:

- ***You Need to Figure Out Who You Would Like to Speak To (Who)*** - Who are you talking to? This question needs to be answered before you come up with any kind of marketing campaign or catch-y tagline. If you don't know who you are talking to specifically, how would you know what you need to say?

- ***What Problem Are You Trying to Solve? (What)*** - What pain point does your business aim to solve with the products and services that you sell? Who are the customers out there with the same kind of problem? The customers who are looking for a product like yours to help them solve this pain point? That will tell you who your niche market is and the group that you should be targeting. There is a good chance that your product or service could solve more than one problem. If that is the case, what you should do as you try to pinpoint your niche in the early stages is to narrow it to one core problem that you want to focus on.

- ***Be Specific About Your Benefits (Why)*** - When crafting out your marketing message for your niche audience, you need to highlight the benefits of your products. Why should your customer be buying from you? How is your product going to change their life for the better? If the benefit of your product is something that is only found within your product, you should highlight this point when marketing to your niche.

- *Brainstorm Who Will Be the Most Interested in Your Products* - Talk to like-minded business friends who could give you some other insight, or perhaps even more ideas, maybe even have a brainstorming session or two with them. Talk to friends and family who are supportive because they too may be able to come up with some pretty good ideas that you could work with. Brainstorming sessions should be done as often as you feel it is necessary. Set a time for it, block out your calendar for a couple of hours to commit to this brainstorming focus entirely on that. Write down everything you know about possible session, and niche options, list them down in order of competition, loyalty, pricing, returns, and more. Compare and contrast which niche is going to give you the best returns, and you may have your answer in front of you on those pieces of paper where you just poured out all your ideas.

- *Have You Tried Looking on Amazon?* - As one of the biggest retailers in the world, Amazon sells just about everything on its platform. Thanks to the presence and reputation it has built for itself over the years, this is now one of the best platforms that you could use at your disposal to find a profitable niche market for your own business. Searching for a potential niche on Amazon is easy. All you would need to do is simply click the "All" tab that is located on the left side of the main search bar, and from there, you will easily find a list of categories which you can select from. Simply find a niche category that grabs your interest, click the "Go" button, and wait for the new page to pop up. On the left side of that page, you will then see the option to select a "sub-niche" category, and by clicking that link, you will be able to view even more specific sub-niches. It's a great platform to source for potential options, and the best part is you will be able to view which products are doing and selling well. Searching for best-selling products is easy. All you would need to do is click on the "Best Sellers" tab from the navigation bar, and there you go.

Chapter 7: Step 7 - Build an Unforgettable Presence

If we strike small talk with a random person, and we find the conversation stimulating and interesting, it will often lead to a full-blown conversation. This is a face-to-face scenario, and more often than not, face-to-face conversations get a little bit more time to convince the other person to listen to you but online communication? Communication on social media? Well, that's another story entirely.

You see, getting someone's attention on social media, or specifically getting your target user's attention on social media is much harder than approaching them and talking to them. Average users only need 8 seconds before they decide the content, they are viewing is not for them. This ultimately means that your conversations on social media not only has to be engaging, it also has to be dynamic and diverse. In short, you need to stand out. You need to give your users a lasting and unforgettable presence.

The Importance of Social Media Presence

Why is it so important to create an unforgettable presence on social media?

Here's why:

- Consumers do not want regurgitated thoughts. They are not looking for flashy promises or empty content.
- Consumers want real value, originality, and excitement.
- They are looking for content that helps them solve their problems.
- They want to make purchasing decisions on what excites them, what helps them solve a problem.
- According to a study done by NewsCred, 62% of millennials say that their loyalty to a brand is directly connected to the quality of the content that the brands they follow produce.

Keep in mind that millennials have been found to spend $200 billion on annual expenditure. This is an extremely important statistic for marketers to keep in mind.

- It's no more about churning out anything just to have something online.
- You need to dedicate content that relates to your business, supports your brand loyalty, and builds your reputation.
- You want to create an unforgettable social media presence so that you are on the top of your consumer's mind the next time they need their problems solved.
- An unforgotten presence ensures continuous growth and effective communication.
- Your consumers are smart and they are not looking for wishy-washy crud or mediocre posts.

In a high-stakes environment where it is harder than ever before to earn attention online, companies must stand out with EPIC content-superb and well-researched material that adds value solves a customer's problem, and has high quality and relevance.

The Benefits of Being Unforgettable

So, what does quality content bring for the marketer and their brand? What are the benefits of being unforgettable on social media?

The effort we put into our content, our look, and the tone of our brand voice and messaging has everything to do with the bottom line-we want profits, and the only way to make profits is to stand out, and the way to stand out is to create epic content.

Being unforgettable on social media brings in more benefits other than increasing our bottom line. Here are some of them:

- More people will talk about you. It'll earn you more shares online, even get you trending.
- You'll have a better reach of your followers- it'll give you a more relevant, exciting, and actionable data to create better content.
- Being unforgettable online lasts longer and is valuable than ordinary content.

- You reach out to a wider pool of people who have stronger brand loyalty and trust in your company.
- Your brand stands out as a thought leader.
- You get to see how adding that extra time and effort into producing. valuable content produced visible results.
- Boring content doesn't produce results, leaving you wondering where you went wrong.

How Do You Make a Lasting Impression?

You probably have an idea of the regular things marketers do to stand out. It is hard to come up with epic content consistently but there are a few things you can do to stay on top and stay unforgettable, and these are the kinds of things that big brands do anyway on a daily basis.

Here they are:

Define Yourself Online-Develop a Consistent Message, Voice, Look and Feel

Consistently sharing and defining your unique message is extremely relevant and valuable to your target audience. You stand out before your brand look & feel is different, but you also stand out because of the language you use to speak to your audience.

Having a consistent message for your brand will enable users to easily identify you from all that clutter and noise. Everything about your online presence needs to be consistent, from your website to your social media channels, your packaging, layout, and even your online banner ads. Consumers need to recognize you instantly.

You do not want your consumers guessing 'who is this brand?' with every message you post out.

Success in being unforgettable leaves no doubt in the consumer's mind- they know who you are, what you care about, and what your values are. It doesn't matter whether they see your logo on a digital banner or on a billboard.

Keep in mind that these values are not only for big businesses. Whether you are a small business owner, entrepreneur, writer, speaker, or budding business, you need to control the narrative in and around your personal brand.

Build a Captivating Social Media Profile

The wonderful thing about social media profiles is that it helps brands present their stories and messages in a fun, creative, and relatable way. These social media platforms also feed data to search engines. Pinpointing your right target audience, who they are, and what they do so you can craft relevant messages is extremely crucial. This makes it easier for your target audience to find you online.

Use every bit of online retail space as best as possible, whether it's on Pinterest or Google+, Instagram, or even the app store. You want to rock your social media profiles with these important points:

- Make sure you tell people who are as simple and as easy as possible. Don't make them guess. A little creativity goes a long way.
- Add links to your blog, website, or any other place you want your consumers to go to.
- Make your profile relatable, accessible, and authentic- these short sentences should be able to tell a story to the search engines as well as to your audience.

Be Authentic

Nobody said you had to be serious all the time- depending on the context. This really depends on how you want to use your brand and leverage on the context and look and feel you're going for. A summary of yourself, your brand, and what you offer has to be authentic so that your audience relates to you.

When you share something authentic, little facts and tidbits about yourself, your past, your struggle, or even your brand, you end up sparking a conversation. People want to know more about you. The fact that you've struggled in your business or had an embarrassing moment happen makes you human, and that appeals to people who have been through a similar situation. Just when your target audience thought you were not relatable, sharing this little info has enabled them to feel a little closer to you and relate to your voice.

Going Organic

Organic growth is the most sustainable of all. Using relevant keywords in an organic way pushes forth a longer, sustainable outcome. You need to dig deep to find out what terms people search for when they look up the niche you are in, the business pool you operate in as well as the product and service you provide. This information should be sewed into your posts, your content, and your keywords.

Google is eager to search and push the story you want to sell so make sure you help Google find you but adding relevant keywords to create a situation that makes it easy to find you and locate you.

Add in Specific Keywords

Keywords are relevant but they do not create the entirety of the solution. Content sells and adding specific keywords that enable you to stand out in your local area, where customers can reach you easily especially if your product or service is a physical one- is extremely crucial.

- ### *Add Your Call-to-Action*

So, you have your presence set and going on fire, but it will all turn to dust if you do not have a call-to-action to direct your customers to a specific goal you want them to do. Where do you want them to go after viewing your content? What do you want them to click on? Having no place to direct your customers is like getting all dressed up and nowhere to go. Make sure there is a call-to-action on whatever content you are putting out there.

- ***Find Your Uniqueness***

Plenty of successful content creators have found the "one thing" that is their unique identity, that one thing that sells them, that one thing that sets them apart. What's yours? If you haven't figured it out yet, it's ok. As long as you keep working on it, the ideas or the image will become more prevalent. Working with your uniqueness will challenge, excite, and inspire you to continue pushing forth and overcoming whatever challenges there may be.

Conclusion

Thank you for making it through to the end of *Social Media Marketing*, let's hope it was informative and able to provide you with all the tools you need to achieve your goals whatever they may be.

There is no doubt about it, the right social media marketing strategy is going to change your business in ways that you cannot even imagine. There is no better way to build your presence in the digital space than through the immense power of social media. This is one brand awareness and sales tool that you cannot afford to pass up on. Not if you are serious about scaling your business to greater heights, that is.

Social media is a wonderful tool, but it can also prove to be a challenging tool if you don't know where to start. It could also be just as challenging if you are someone who wears multiple hats in your business. Whether your business is big or small, you need social media on your side, that much is clear. Even if you are juggling multiple roles in your business, the key is to identify what aspects of social media you should be focused on to better drive your business. Everything that matters has been covered in this guide. The only thing that is left is for you to get started.

Social media marketing is going to be the very thing that takes your business from mediocre to number one. You want profits, and the only way to make profits is to stand out and the way to stand out is to create epic content, and target the right people with the right strategies. Make a commitment to social media. Make social media marketing a priority for you and your business. Start by planning, create your strategy, create your goals, and identify what success looks like to you. Establish some goals for your social media marketing, and the best thing you can do for your business is to develop goals that align with your social media strategy. Don't forget to be as specific as possible with the details.

Book 3: Content Marketing

7 Easy Steps to Master Content Strategy, Content Creation, Search Engine Optimization & Copywriting

Santino Spencer

Introduction

Welcome to *Content Marketing*. As with many undertakings in life, you can't attain your full potential for success with content marketing until you precisely understand what it is. How content marketing is defined, what business goals it can assuage you in achieving, and what positions unique content should play in relevance to your other marketing routines and strategies are other areas we will cover in this guide. When you offer a strategic approach to the creation and dissemination of relevant and consistent material to capture the attention of a clearly defined target group, content marketing will be the engine of customer actions.

Compared with the typical sales technique of pitching your products or services to your potential customers, content marketing achieves results by snaring your target audience's attention. Furthermore, content marketing addresses your prospects' needs for information and guides them to a specific conclusion. Over time, the notion is that they will come to trust and rely on your guidance, recognize your company's peerless value proposition, and when all is said and done, reward you with their business and brand allegiance.

This guide will focus on the "how-to" creation and distribution of content marketing, using narratives with an emotional appeal as a way to engage and educate customers and prospects in order to build long-term relationships with human connections, and create sales success. In a seven-step process, you will understand the purpose of attracting finely defined audiences and building content that will lead to credibility, trust, and potential sales.

In a nutshell, for content marketing to be successful, it must offer relevance to a target audience, provide that audience with tangible value, and maintain consistency throughout all messaging.

As outlined in this guide, these three goals can be reached when specific steps are followed and adhered to with pragmatism, strategy, and alignment with the standards of quality, value, and the purpose your audience expects. Let's get started!

Chapter 1: Step 1 - Understand the Value Proposition

Content marketing is not a new concept.

A case in point is "Poor Richard's Almanack," a collection of all sorts of interesting information, such as; a calendar, weather predictions, sayings, poems, recipes, and advice. Benjamin Franklin began publishing his almanac in 1732 to promote his printing business and published it for 25 years. By providing his almanac readers with a variety of exciting information, Franklin gained their trust, and, in turn, his dedicated readers purchased his print services.

Content marketing is a viable strategy that includes developing original, pertinent content for your business associates, customers, and prospects. A long-term plan, content marketing contains all marketing formats that involve creating and sharing content with the primary purpose of acquiring and engaging your audience.

Content needs to accomplish much more than simply loading up on information. It has to build trust among your current and prospective clients while creating brand awareness that makes your website much more visible so that additional information about your value proposition is the main attraction.

Leverage Existing Content

Employing existing content will result in a low cost compared with advertising and public relations.

Content marketing goes far beyond simply writing. When you leverage existing content and create new content for marketing purposes, more leads and increased sales should result. Additionally, updating your search engine optimization, so your audience experiences your innovative content should manifest better relationships with your customers.

People who excel as content marketers are excellent communicators with a skill set in writing succinctly and effectively. Being a savvy marketer is a highly desirable quality to possess. Being savvy enables you to keep customers' aims in mind while harmonizing them with business objectives. The most skilled marketers know how to take data and process it so that it can be used to track progress and provide feedback for marketing efforts.

When done correctly, compelling content all but guarantees a relationship with your audience, ultimately leading to trust. When your audience members trust you, they're more willing to do business with you when they are ready to make a purchasing decision. When you are looking to cultivate the art of communicating with your prospects without pitching your product or service, look at content marketing as the logical solution.

Marketers should specially design content for the primary purpose of educating their visitors.

Think about it this way:

A curious visitor lands on your website in search of answers to their queries. By offering an adequate mix of content and information, you provide your readers with what they need and build a long-lasting relationship with them. Experience informs us that people return to websites that they can trust, compelled to visit those websites to garner as much knowledge as possible. When you consistently and regularly add great content, you will engage your audience, which will provide a win-win situation for you, your prospects, and existing customers.

The onslaught of advertising messages is so overwhelming that audiences are flinching, building a form of "attention surveillance" against ads. While consumers may have once looked to advertising as a way to stay informed about products and services, objective information proliferates the Internet. With the consumer in control, people are turning ads off. Whether fast-forwarding on digital recording or installing ad blocking software in their browsers, consumers arm themselves with technology in the war for their attention.

Engage Your Audience

Increasingly, they're turning to a new strategy: content marketing. Rather than produce congratulatory ads about their products, effective marketers know how to publish content that engages or entertains prospects-sometimes, without any overt reference to the company's products. It's a paradigm shift for many marketers – but the phenomenon of thinking "like a journalist" is beginning to take root in many of the world's best-known brands.

Content marketing is the best way that you can foster brand awareness for new target consumers. Marketers can do it at a fraction of advertising costs. Compared with fostering visibility for your brand by way of traditional advertising, which could be quite costly, content marketing provides businesses with a much-needed change in mindset. And, when done correctly, appropriate content can seem a magical solution to promoting visibility and traffic for your website. It enables new customers to get to know your brand though they may not have heard of it before. Unique and clever content can provide consumers with the opportunity to discover new products and services that provide value-- compelling them to return time and time again.

The real value proposition enters the picture with storytelling, and we all know, everyone loves a good narrative. Storytelling connects people to a group, gives us a reason to communicate, and provides relevance. Stories offer us something to believe in and make us feel loved, safe, and smarter—great content is about establishing alignment between your business, customers, and prospects.

You have to remember, though, that telling the story of your brand is more than your website content, your blog, white papers, or even social media. It's all about how you convey your value, mission, and how you consistently communicate with them over the long term.

We now know that our content must attract the right people to your site, engage those people into leads, and nurture and help close them into customers. But remember, your job doesn't end there. Your content should also continue to delight your customers and turn them into brand ambassadors for your product or service.

Great content is not promotional. Top-notch content must excite and inspire, both critical components of the kind of content used to drive brand awareness. Non-specific content that is not quite related to your target audience may not deliver results. When crafting your materials, you need to ensure that they will be useful to your reader.

Concrete, unique content must close a gap-it should answer a business question. If you offer information that doesn't resonate with the audience, it will fall upon deaf ears.

Creative content must be carefully written. If you present poorly produced content, it may end up hurting the brand's overall perception.

It is imperative that your content supports business objectives and is relevant to your organization. If not, it may result in a waste of valuable resources. Therefore, please ensure to keep your business' goals focused when producing content and be aware that your content might be biased. After all, it is your business, so make sure that you know how to develop content that offers proof and validation through customer reviews and comments in addition to real metrics and data.

Your content should exude self-confidence, trustworthiness, and reliability to ensure that your audience visits your website frequently. As you learn how to develop reliable content and your audience believes in you, you have reached the pinnacle and acquired your fan base. Once achieved, sharing more and more content with your regular and loyal followers, the better your relationship with them becomes. This will lead to an unshakable marketing strategy.

Tailor Your Content

A content creator or content marketing service provider will adjust appropriate content to resonate with the intended audience. While using different formats, including blog posts, newsletters, infographics, e-Books, podcasts, and YouTube videos, etc., the purpose of content creation is to communicate a message to your desired audience. Content marketing uses that content to meet your business's marketing goals, such as; acquiring potential customers, retaining existing ones, and raising awareness about your brand, product, or service.

Capturing audiences and growing revenue are but two of the benefits of content marketing. Content marketers cannot measure results purely in monetary terms. With its explosive growth and no signs of lagging, content marketing will grow faster with a guarantee of staying around for a very long time. The deciding factor between business success and failure will rest at the feet of online content marketing. Digital marketers will realize that one cannot merely skip content marketing. It must remain an integral component of their digital marketing arsenal if they need to succeed.

Chapter 2: Step 2 - Build the Narrative with Content Marketing

This chapter will teach us about storytelling and the reasons why it's highly useful for marketing. We will also discuss the best practices for your business' marketing through amazing storytelling efforts.

So, what exactly is a story?

In this approach, you create a narrative based on real or fictional characters around events described for entertainment purposes. As such, storytelling is all about creating a narrative. The narrative must convey a clear message to the intended audience. A good story revolves around the main character in addition to other secondary personas, a central plot, some conflicts, obstacles, customers, and pain points, a central theme that follows throughout the story, and a narrative arc.

From our earliest beginnings, oral storytelling was a method used by cavemen to communicate, educate, share, and connect, while ancient Egyptians used hieroglyphics for the same purpose. Throughout history, stories have captured a special place in our lives. A great narrative ought to be catchy, clearly apparent, credible, authentic, useful, inclusive, and inspiring. When these elements make up the story – brands can use storytelling to help audiences understand how their products provide value in their lives.

A prime example is Subaru's ads, which communicate "love" through a series of ads, telling stories that immortalize the car brand as a symbol of caring and concern for those you love. Whether it's a father's concern for his son or daughter, or a parent caring for their beloved pet, the series of ads provide compelling stories, telling us what the brand represents to the family and not the horsepower that the car delivers. Using this innovative way of weaving a narrative through its brand's stories, Subaru elevates its meaning and better shows how it fits into customers' desired lifestyles.

The Power Tool

Storytelling is a content marketer's power tool. It helps bring a deeper meaning and a stronger connection with your target audience and adds an element of humanity to your content, and, therefore, your brand. Telling stories through your content exceeds mere advertising. It ought to compel audiences to confide in your brand much more easily.

Content marketers should implement storytelling into their marketing strategy narratives to relay an idea. The aim is to produce a feeling in your audience. It ought to be enough to compel them to act, preferably making a purchase, or any other kind of action. Thus, using storytelling as a marketing tool gives consumers an understanding of why they should focus on something while highlighting your brand's value.

When a content marketer introduces storytelling into their organization, positive and empathy-inducing effects can be experienced, with the added results of better understanding customers, arming sales teams, getting bigger budgets, and even illuminating a company's culture.

Marketers need a solid foundation in understanding empathy before they try and sell anything to anyone. Relating to your customer in this way can make the difference between a well-received campaign and a disastrous outcome.

Creating Customer Identities

One of the most discernable settings in which we deploy storytelling in a marketing strategy is creating customer identities. We do this by interviewing customers so we may tell real and meaningful life stories. Once accomplished, we can build characters and focus on our customers' pain points and challenges. Then, we can imagine what our organization can do to help them succeed. We want our target audience to be the heroes of their own stories.

Why Do We Do This?

To generate a result and get your audience to respond to your story's message and take action. However, your audience won't look at your narrative or react to your account if it is not relevant. For your story to be appropriate, you have to understand what matters to your target audience and what difficulties they are experiencing in order to show them how you will relieve their pain. It comes down to your ability to empathize with them.

Scientific evidence supports the notion that a boost to our oxytocin levels, a hormone that creates positive feelings in an individual such as love, union, and pleasure, in the brain occurs as a result of telling emotional and character-driven stories. The product is a feeling of empathy. The human mind is wired to latch on to consistent narratives.

So, What Do Marketers Seek to Get from Their Efforts?

A healthy and positive connection with their audience. Storytelling can foster that relationship as 92 percent of target audiences want their ads to feel like stories.

Because of this proof, the best marketers know that leveraging the power of storytelling improves branding. These narratives also increase conversion rates from prospective customers to actual customers by 30 percent. People remember stories 22- times more than data consisting of facts and figures.

Cutting Through the Clutter

As more brands move toward content marketing, cutting through the clutter is more vital than ever before. But our brains, after all, are built to connect with compelling stories.

Storytelling is an essential strategic tool; it can be a crucial tactical method that lets marketers encourage consumers' engagement in a splintered media world. Because of the trend in increasing choice and consumption of a range of media and the increased difficulty in reaching target audiences, consumers are demanding different and unique experiences and different ways of receiving their content. Consumers are no longer willing to give you their time without something enticing in exchange. Storytelling isn't just a creative marketing approach. You need to provide your consumers with a separate entry to your brand.

Benefits of Storytelling

Storytelling is an absolute necessity for successful content marketing because:

- A more profound and solid connection with recipients is achievable.
- It provides a humanistic touch to your materials and, therefore, your brand.

- People trust your brand more readily because good storytelling goes beyond advertising.

- A business with a great story can easily overcome competition.

- Stories are the most successful weapon when you are looking to create brand loyalty. Reliable content marketing in narratives translates into people becoming much likelier to recommend your brand or product through word-of-mouth advertising. After all, it is the best manner to get a brand's story in front of the masses.

Principles of Storytelling

To transform your ordinary product or service into something exemplary in the minds of your target audience, you must advertise your business with eye-catching stories. To do this successfully, experts recommend that you follow six basic principles of storytelling:

1. *Identify a Relatable Main Character*

This protagonist ought to be a persona in the narrative that audiences can identify with. This character needs to be appealing, exciting, and well defined so that the narrative makes a strong impression in the minds of your target audience. Your entire story revolves around this character, so it's a crucial role in your development.

2. *Place the Best Parts of Your Story at the Beginning*

Just as you would write any narrative or article, the great hook comes first so you can lure your reader in from the get-go.

3. *Add Conflict*

A conflict has news value and will keep your audience engaged. This conflict or obstacle could relate to the characters of the story who either don't get what they want or don't, and something else bad happens, or they get what they want, and something goes askew as a result.

4. *Maintain Authenticity*

People connect with authentic people. Your story must be genuine and unique and stay loyal to your brand, so people will react and connect to your tale with ease. Keep it simple and zero in on a single issue and have a conclusion at the end.

5. *Incorporate Your Innovative Selling Point*

Use the story's power to educate and persuade people that your product is the best with data and research to validate your suggestions.

6. *Give Your Story Three Actions*

An intriguing brand story needs three parts that present the scenario, describe the conflict, and show the conclusion. Remember that each story should be unique to the business as they require a fourth part, a clear call to action.

Transmit Knowledge and Meaning

Storytelling is also a powerful method for learning for content marketers. We should always seek to understand more about the world we live in, the brands that we represent, and the audiences we serve. One of the unique aspects of stories is that they transmit knowledge and meaning. As marketers, we learn from observations, first-hand experiences, and then, share those experiences through words and actions in our narratives. Storytelling is a vital tool that allows marketers to understand what is taking place in the marketplace and what that meaning translates to the customer, consumer, society, brand, and company.

There is a reason stories captivate us. As children and through adulthood, the lessons we internalize mold us. The wonderful adventures that we go on, the knowledge we gain, and the possibilities afforded allow us to unfold our imaginations.

Stories are used to highlight our culture. As such, narratives provide evidence of the lives we have lived. Stories are also used to hand down wisdom more easily. That is why storytelling is the oldest way we transmit information. We are influenced tremendously by how we view and interpret those things we like to call facts.

When you provide your products and services with a clear identity, you do so through the stories you share. By taking your intended audience on a trip that satisfies their need for adventure and experience. In this way, consumers can establish a personal bond with your brand. Consequently, your narrative must be real, creative, and motivational.

To produce your narrative, you ought to illustrate your tone, that is what you believe in, and the reason why your audience's experience will be better because of it.

Many media platforms are at your disposal to paint your narrative. For instance, video, blogs, print materials, websites, and social media platforms. All these media bring about a different reaction from your followers. As such, tales need to be tailored for each group. When you know which story to tell and which medium to use for its distribution, you have achieved success. Short, crisp vignette-style narratives are better suited for television and online platforms whereas online talks, seminars, and shows deliver more intimate connections.

As we have learned about the importance of storytelling in content marketing, we now see that a brand relies on perception. To create a narrative that hits home with social issues, you must produce a condition that connects emotionally with your audience. Consequently, emotional marketing constitutes a modern advertising approach that shows potential to increase earnings and customer retention along with long-term customer relationships – all the things you want to move your business to success. As such, the way that someone feels about your brand is what generally establishes if they purchase your products or not.

Chapter 3: Step 3 - Structure Influence and Authority

In previous chapters, we have discussed how content marketing is centered on increasing revenues as a result of providing consumers with the value they have been looking for.

Within the cluttered highway of constant bombardment with traditional advertising, content marketing presents a great chance to quiet the chatter and offer real value to our consumers.

We know that content marketing can drive more sales; however, most of your customers follow a buying process before they make a purchase. In the initial stage, your target audience needs to understand they have a need that requires a solution. This is what promotes awareness. So, customers can take the opportunity to research and obtain knowledge to inform them about the situation better – that's a consideration. Then, they determine which solution is the best way for them to solve their problem—this is where they can make a decision.

A solidly built marketing plan aids your potential consumers throughout the three parts of the sales funnel.

Boundless Benefits

The benefits of content marketing are infinite. Here are some of those benefits:

Improve and Drive Conversions

Research tells us that those enterprises that produce consistent marketing content experience the benefit of converting a prospect at a sixfold rate as compared to their competitors that don't pay attention to content marketing. Good content helps to bring your potential customers one step closer to making a purchase.

Build Authority

Solid and well-placed content helps to build a relationship and also to make your target audience more likely to work with your business instead of your competitors. As you produce high-quality content that offers value to your audience, you begin to accrue credibility and a reputation as an authority figure. Writing content about your specific industry challenges your customers to face issues that relate to them. Once you have garnered their trust, this will compel folks to seek your expertise and knowledge regarding your products or services in order to offer value to their current situation. Your materials will enable you to take advantage of the positive outcomes stemming from content marketing.

Social Media Enhancement

When a prospective customer finds valuable content on your site, they transform into a potential advocate for your brand, and, in turn, they will pass your content's message to their friends and family on social media. Your following will grow exponentially over time. We have seen the expanse of power that social media marketing has in capturing and connecting with new leads while nurturing time-honored alliances with your existing clients. When your content consists of beneficial information, it is a good idea to be prolific across your social media presence. As your customers discover the value your material provides, they will feel compelled to follow your brand across the social media channels your content exists.

Lead Generation

Generating more on-site content, which, in turn, gives you more content, provides your customers with more reasons to visit your site, more opportunities to get to know your value proposition, and greater confidence, thereby leading to more conversions to actual sales.

Assisting Your Customer Service and Sales Teams

Ease the burden on your customer service and sales team by providing an FAQ of frequently asked questions, compiled in a blog post, or on your website. Many items that customers or prospects might ask are usually standard, have been asked before, and are easy to answer in one central location on your website. Often, people use Google to obtain their answers, and then, if users cannot get the answers they seek, your audience may reach out to your company directly.

As we know, most questions are redundant and have been asked a myriad of times. Why not set your customer service and sales teams free to do more critical work? Reduce their workload and inquiries by posting these standard questions and answers for ready accessibility.

Amplifying Your Brand Awareness and Affinity

This is where consumers feel passionate about and share the values of a company's brand. They love what you sell, frequently tell their friends and family about how great you are, and will talk up your products or services without prompting or coercion. They are your super fans and, no doubt, your most valuable customers.

Educate Your Customers

Your current customers and prospects are experiencing a pain point, and your brand can solve their problems. When you produce materials based on your customers' most significant issues, you improve your comprehension of what they need so that they can find effective solutions to their issues.

Cost-Effectiveness

Value and results might not be evident for several months, but after that, the growth can be exponential when done right. Since it is generally simpler, to begin with, the most popular options capitalize on audiences that are bored of the same types of content. As such, content marketing can aid in monetizing clever angles that marketing specialists need to utilize in the pursuit of potential customers.

It is a well-known fact that traditional advertising methods, including radio, TV, billboards, print, etc., are more costly than content in the form of blog posts, visuals, white papers, social media, etc. And the most significant advantage that content marketing offers compared with traditional advertising is that the net results are straightforward to measure.

The impact of a TV or print ad, poster, a billboard is often impossible to benchmark. That has always been one of the "cons" of traditional advertising, and metrics are vital to determine your campaigns' success. Conversely, it is relatively easy to measure your blog posts' success, etc., and other forms of content marketing.

There is also a lifetime or evergreen factor to consider, and that lifetime value doesn't exist with traditional advertising. Your website or blog posts' content continues with longevity and drives traffic in perpetuity unless you get rid of it.

Yes, it's a gradual process and requires time, as the results accumulate over time, often the only real investment requires - time.

Content marketers might not see tremendous results during the first several months. But over time, your material will begin to produce more and more. This is why traditional marketing is considered to be a temporary effort.

Enhance SEO efforts

Content marketing provides higher visibility (Step 3) in search engines since consumers utilize search engines to research products or services. Audiences utilize online searches when looking for information on products and services.

Search engine optimization or SEO optimizes your site's placement in search results across the various engines available.

It's relatively simple. Your SEO position or ranking in Google, Excite, Yahoo!, Bing, Ask.com, AOL, or DuckDuckGo, will improve with better quality content. So, your SEO is better based on your quality content. So, suppose someone searches for "What is content management software?" On Google or any other search engine. In that case, they find your blog presented with the words contained in the title. A higher search engine ranking helps draw this curious individual to your site so they can find out more and discover more about your brand and how it can help provide answers to your questions and offer solutions for your pain points.

Higher Domain Authority

Better quality content augments the way folks perceive your expertise, power, importance, and confidence in your webpage. Your website's rankings are a reflection of your domain's popularity. As such, the more high-quality material you generate, your materials gain more incoming links for other sources. This enhanced domain authority matches up with greater visibility. This positively impacts your entire website providing you with an enviable position in the content marketing realm.

Universal Application

Content marketing can prove beneficial for corporations in all fields across a myriad of industries. Content marketers will achieve success when they find the appropriate materials and types of content that resonate with the intended audience. Content marketing is generally unique. As such, any company in any field can benefit from it.

Less Rankling and Intrusive Than Traditional Advertising

Every day, we are inundated with a barrage of ads. Research indicates that at least 50% of folks have some kind of ad filter installed in their internet browser. So, give some thought to the notion that if you can't deliver an ad because potential customers won't see it, how can an advertisement build sales? It can't.

This is precisely the point at which content marketing makes a difference. It is not as annoying as it seems much more natural in the way information is presented.

We hope these twelve benefits of content marketing motivate you to create new, unique content. Remember to be authentic, show your brand personality, and establish your tone of voice in each piece of content you share.

This means that content marketing is not merely fleeting. In our current online world, this type of advertising is crucial. Whether you're seeking accelerated web hits, improved conversion numbers, or healthier connections with your current consumers, content marketing, a mission-critical growth method for all businesses, must hold a strategic place in your marketing arsenal.

More and more organizations are jumping on the bandwagon and moving toward developing a content marketing strategy for their business and embarking on a program to produce great materials for their products or services.

The size of your company or industry isn't an issue. You start to implement a content approach right away to reach your intended audience, resolve their pain points, and convert them into loyal customers perpetuating your brand.

Chapter 4: Step 4 - Build and Strategize

We've established that content marketing is useful to reach your customers and grow your business in the preceding chapters. We now know it's a magnificent way to raise awareness for your value proposition among your intended followers so that your marketing endeavors can position you online, improve web hits, generate leads, and close sales.

There's a challenge, though. Reaping a content marketing campaign's benefit is not feasible if you lack the proper strategy, approach, and actions. How do I dodge wasting time on the wrong content marketing approach? Evidence shows implementing effective content is a troublesome area for most marketing professionals. As such, many marketing professionals require guidance on constructing an effective content approach.

In this chapter, we will review "how-to" create an ideal content strategy.

Document Your Aims, Goals, Along with Key Performance Indicators

The mission statement is a short account of who your customers are, the way you plan to engage them, and how they stand to profit from your materials. It is often similar if not identical to the "About Us" section of a press release or press kit. Goals are equally essential to include in your content strategy as goals help define what you expect to derive from your marketing endeavors. A simple way to approach the development of your goals might be to think of it as you provide your [target audience-who are they?] with a [type of content-what is it?] to help them achieve their [business goals-what do they need from you for you to achieve your goal?]. We touched upon some specific plans in previous chapters, but worth reiterating include increasing sales, getting more qualified leads, and increasing traffic to your website.

Key performance indicators (KPIs) that determine your marketing strategy help you achieve your business goals. Every digital marketing campaign need KPIs. Most of the time, profitability is a critical factor in measuring KPIs. Different businesses use content in a variety of ways; your KPIs might vary accordingly. Most companies are primarily interested in revenue, sales, ROI, and purchases directly generated from social media. One way to simplify KPIs is to realize that the essential metrics measure sales and revenue; basically, how much money a company is making based on their KPIs. There are too many other variables for KPIs to include here. However, for your review, much is written on the subject.

1. Know Your Audience

To build a perfect content strategy, you need to know the audience to whom you are marketing. Familiarity with your audience helps tremendously in targeting your content appropriately. We've already learned that marketing will only work if the content is relevant to your audience. If you produce materials thinking about a sweeping approach, your content will not resonate with anyone.

An inception moment should include research; obtaining those demographics using the web, social media, and web analytics data. You will identify the various demographic indicators that comprise your audience. You ought to collect feedback from followers to help you visualize their needs and pain points, determine what platform to use best in order to reach them, and identify the ideal customer persona. When all of these elements come together, you will know which materials to produce, how these will provide value, and how they will resonate with your audience.

2. Plan Your Process

You must plan the content creation process, including:

- What resources do you need for content creation?
- What your content production workflow is?
- What your publishing schedule is?
- Who has final content approval?
- Who is in charge of creating content?

- Who will be accountable for maintaining and updating content?

3. Create a Blog

Blogs tend to be the core of a solid strategy. It's the portal or hub for all other content marketing efforts and is considered by experts to be a vital component of a marketing approach. If you haven't created a blog, now is the time. Some ideas for blog posts might include:

- A glance behind the curtain
- Answer "Why?"
- Beginner's guides
- Case studies
- Checklists
- Comparisons
- Conference posts
- Contests
- Controversial subjects
- Debates
- Event summaries
- Expert advice
- FAQs
- Find funny videos for blog posts
- Free giveaways
- Funny posts
- Guest bloggers

- How-to guides
- Industry news and insights
- Infographics
- Inspirational stories
- Interviews
- Lifestyle posts
- Listicles (yes, a list of articles, including links)
- Local news (non-business related)
- Metrics to measure guides
- Monthly updates and stats
- MP3s
- Myth vs. fact
- Parody posts
- Personal stories
- Pop-culture commentary
- Presentations and SlideShare
- Preview posts of what's coming next
- Problems and solutions
- Profiles
- Questions you should be asking
- Quizzes
- Rants
- Recent tools you use
- Resources
- Reviews

- Roundups
- Screencasts
- Share what others are saying
- Surveys and polls
- Think out loud posts
- Timesaving ideas
- Top takeaways from whatever
- Transcript posts from conferences, webinars
- Tutorials
- Twitter posts
- Upcoming events
- Video blogs
- White papers

Your blog posts must be:

- Controversial
- Educational
- Fun
- Useful

Audit Your Existing Content

If you already have content, you must determine if you are achieving your targets and delivering on your key performance indicators (KPIs). You can do this by auditing your content. There's a three-step process you can follow:

1. Keep track of what you've got
2. Determine if it's working
3. Searching for missing areas

You can do this with a website crawler that is capable of analyzing results in real-time. Free tools are available that will allow you to crawl URLs to identify broken links, redirect errors, index your webpages, generate XML sitemaps, etc.; however, for a good one, you will have to make a purchase. Paid products of this type will enable you to schedule crawling, save crawling results, custom extractions from the website coding, JS rendering, Google Webmaster tools integration, etc. And, for complex businesses, with multiple blogs, etc., you might have to do this. For our purposes in this "how-to" guide, look into **Xenu's Link Sleuth**.

This web-scraping software checks for broken links on sites and refreshes them. Broken links can negatively impact your search engine ranking. Xenu supports both SSL and FTP sites and reports on all broken and redirected URLs.

Research Keywords and Create Content

A vital aspect of generating content is to research keywords. Since you are keen on having folks find your content, you want to compel them to visit your site. As such, keywords are items that folks use to find online content. These are the terms that people enter in Google, or any other search engine, to find what they are looking for.

There are three elemental keywords that you need to include in your content are:

1. General search items, or keywords, that identify a general topic or concept, such as "document storage."
2. Medium length search terms that are comprised of three or more keywords that narrow the search down, such as "document storage facilities.
3. Full phrases that include several keywords, such as "document storage facilities nearby."

The fewer words, the higher the cost and competition and lower probability of conversion; the more info, the lower the cost and risk and the higher likelihood of conversion

The right keywords are crucial in your content since they help search engines like Google link your content with what the searchers are investigating. Keywords guide your audience from a simple, initial **navigational** stage where prospects are on a search for a specific or several specific sites. Then, they move to the **educational** stage, seeking answers to their questions about their need(s). Finally, they go to the **investigational** stage, where they are narrowing down their final choice(s) in their pre-purchase options, to finally, the **transactional** stage, where your prospects are ready to buy. Whether it's a business enterprise or an individual consumer, in these modern times, this is how consumers search for what they want.

Your keywords must perfectly align with your business, so your target audience will arrive at your website following these three stages.

Be sure to check **Google Analytics** as well as **Google Search Console** so you can establish which search terms drive the most traffic to your site. Utilize keyword search software to uncover the best keywords to incorporate into your materials. One considered popular and efficient device is **SEMrush**.

Other keyword research tools include:

- Ahrefs
- Answer the Public (basic use is free)
- Bing Webmaster Tools
- Google AdWords Keyword Planner
- Google Trends
- Keyword Eye

- Keyword Spy (free trial)
- Keyword Tool (free)
- Long Tail Pro
- LIS Graph
- Moz Keyword Explorer (free domain SEO metrics)
- SEO Book Keyword Suggestion Tool
- Soovie
- SpyFu
- Ubersuggest
- Wordstream Keyword Tool

Once you have found your perfect keywords, you should strive to incorporate them into your materials in spots that include:

- The name for your content page.
- An SEO-optimized title for your content. It could differ from the title found on your content page.
- Your content's meta description.
- The complete content items.
- It should be found on relevant links to your page.
- Updates on social media regarding your content.

So, do keep these points in mind as they will help you get the most out of your approach.

Finalize Your Lead Magnet or Hook

A lead magnet is also known as a "hook." This is an element that incentivizes customers by offering a potential customer some type of value in order to get their contact information such as email or phone number. Generally speaking, these magnets offer value through free reports, white papers, e-books, free trials, special offers, case studies, webinars, quizzes, or mini-courses.

Lead magnets or hooks increase the conversion rates for lead generation activities. A well-functioning lead magnet must be specific and short-term in nature, solve a real problem, or eliminate pain points for your consumers and offer an alternative that is easy and fast to pursue. Lead magnets ought to provide value, in an easily digestible format that displays your knowledge on the matter.

What adds to an element of the challenge with lead magnets is that emails are very personal, much like a birthday, age, marital status, etc. Most folks won't easily provide you with their contact information unless they receive something they truly perceive as valuable even if your followers are happy with your brand. As an effective content marketing professional, you need to compel your followers to do so.

What makes a good lead magnet or hook, you ask?

Several things can make your lead magnet irresistible and turn a lead into a customer down the road:

- It solves a problem or pain point.
- It promises one quick win and be easy to achieve that win.
- It should be super-specific.
- It should be quick to digest.
- It should be favorably perceived and of actual high value.
- It should be instantly accessible, delivered right away, and provide instant gratification.
- It should clearly show your authority or authentic value proposition.

Commit to a Publishing Schedule

Anyone who uses content as a marketing strategy has likely gone a long time without adding a single word to their content.

For many content writers, extensive writing is a tedious chore. You might enjoy writing, but when working in a full-time job with only a few hours a week available for content development, this task might get relegated to a place far down your job responsibilities.

Setting a goal for how often and how much time you can delegate to producing and publishing your content is the first step. You can then set hard deadlines for the dates you will have to go live with that content.

No doubt, writing content, including blog posts, is time-consuming. First, you need to brainstorm the topic you want to write about, research the case to gather supporting materials to embellish your content, produce the blog post, or other content, and collect images to enhance your materials.

As you produce your content regularly, you should begin to complete it in less time. You will establish your go-to research resources, accumulate images for your post headers that you can reuse from post-to-post, and this will stimulate ideas for future content.

But the first step is first. Set a goal and get that on your calendar, and don't worry about the frequency you choose. Now, you are accountable!

Boost Your Materials

An essential element of your content marketing approach is to boost your materials, so they align with your specific goals. Here, we will explore how you can publicize the content you develop using these three devices.

Social Media Marketing

Social media networks help improve content prominence. Social media marketing is a core element of content marketing. If you target **Bing's** search traffic, it would be helpful to determine how social media is used to rank websites.

To write a catchy headline, you need to use a catchy image on social media and a blog. Please ensure that you use the right keywords so you can improve your site's visibility.

Email Marketing

A very effective way to market with content is through email. You can keep tabs with followers to build positive relationships. The best email content is short, easily readable, provides a good hook, and avoids being directly gimmicky. Most email campaigns yield approximately $40 for everyone you invest. You can't beat those odds!

Link Building

Links are a significant factor in SEO ranking. So, be sure to build those links. An excellent way to begin is establishing who is already linking to you by using one of the audit tools discussed previously.

Links are essential when creating content because they improve the navigation of your site as users find your content. That's a great SEO approach. Linking your best stuff among fresh content is a great habit to follow consistently. Think about returning to your current content over time. Consider linking older content to a newer one. When you link to authoritative, trustworthy external sources, it reflects best on your site and presents you as legitimate, reliable, and trustworthy.

Receiving a good range of inbound links is crucial as well. Some ways to achieve this include:

- Securing reviews and client testimonials for your company, items, and services.
- Requesting folks to help promote your site.
- Finding, addressing, and repairing broken links.
- Guest blogging and participating in expert roundups and interviews.

In closing, we've established that content marketing is beneficial when used correctly to raise awareness of your brand, engage your customers, and boost your company. A successful content marketing campaign can lead to online authority, web traffic, leads, and sales.

The challenge we addressed in this chapter is that reaping a content marketing campaign's benefit is not feasible without a solid content marketing approach, actions, and tools.

Chapter 5: Step 5 - Align Content Marketing with the Buyer's Journey

We've reviewed content marketing, its purposes, mission, value, and benefits in previous chapters. We also learned about building the narrative for content marketing and some ways to promote your company with amazing narratives. Additionally, we understand how utilizing content marketing enables focus on increasing sales by providing customers with the information they are looking for. In Chapter 4, we discovered that no matter how good your content is, you must have the right content marketing strategy in place.

Although most companies understand the advantage of using content-based marketing, many of them head straight into generating and disseminating materials without first building the overall campaign's core foundation.

The critical challenge of jumping right in to produce content has the negative implication that without previous planning and structure, a business won't possess the means of tracking workflow or foresee interactions of content among several various channels, resulting in wasted time and money.

This chapter will identify content mapping and how it must align with the buyer's journey and discover the different sales funnel steps and the implications for positive content marketing.

How does content mapping work toward making your content marketing plan a success?

Content mapping provides an organization with a congruent and structured approach to plan, produce, and assess content from an overall perspective. It provides a clear vision that enables you to plan out and comprehend the way all of your materials interact. You can then establish the structure you require to aid your advertising efforts.

Content mapping is akin to building a **concept map** or a diagram used to organize information visually. It provides a hierarchy and shows relationships among pieces of the whole. A concept map focuses on a site's material as it will enable you to explore and see your content in action.

Concept mapping enables you to view your materials about your client's goals, the intentions of visitors to your site, as well as all other aspects pertaining to your website (and other external sites). You can identify breaches (and chances), in your content creation approach.

Suppose we look at content mapping through the lens of the following analogy. In that case, that your materials are the fuel that moves your marketing approach, and content mapping is the guiding beacon that illuminates your business so you can visualize what you need to do to conduct a beneficial content campaign.

A logical follow-up question might be, what is the purpose of using content mapping?

We know that the best means of capturing our follower's attention is to generate high-quality materials that paint an adventure. In its most simplistic terms, the goals of mapping your content approach are to **create a connection with your followers** so that you can create a two-way interaction with them. The conversation goes through several different stages in which your business' content approach is manifest. The most important aspect to know and follow is that you want to rush your audience at no point in the steps.

The days of the one sale's call approach and the deal is signed, sealed, and delivered are over. Did they ever really exist?

Your customers and prospects are quite picky and sophisticated, so your company needs to establish a connection to gain an advantage over your competitors. When you begin your content marketing process with the creation and execution of a content map, it is necessary to maintain a top-down approach in order to make appropriate content marketing assessments so that you can prepare for upcoming efforts.

Your Content Mapping Approach

A significant component of executing a sound content mapping strategy is that you must align, at each stage, specific content to your audience's needs and desires. The content marketer must frequently review each step (or stage), and continually assess the accuracy of your assumptions and customer preference by receiving consistent customer feedback.

A significant challenge for content mapping is knowing when to transfer an individual from one stage to the next. These "triggers," as they are referred to by content marketing experts, are reliant on various elements, such as:

- Aggressiveness of business
- Industry
- Market segregation
- Product lifecycle
- Price of service or product, distribution, and stock
- The type of sales approach (B2C, B2B, etc.)

It would be best to determine these triggers to layout your materials successfully.

An appropriate way to define the motivations (triggers) is by establishing the effectiveness of the specific paths your followers go on. For instance, you must gauge your email advertising to ascertain who interacts with specific materials. You should apply this same idea to every channel that your followers interact with as this feedback will aid you in transitioning individuals to the next step.

What Are the Benefits of Content Mapping?

Content Mapping Helps You Gain a Better Understanding of Your Customers and Prospects

Hopefully, when you follow the path customers take on their way to doing business with you, you acquire a deeper, more complex understanding of their goals, needs, questions, and pain points. This understanding can help you achieve more successful marketing strategies and improve your target audience's products or services.

Content Mapping Provides an Overview of All of Your Content

With content mapping, you can audit and catalog your existing content. Having one central content repository enables you to avoid creating redundant content and highlights opportunities to reuse or repurpose your current content materials.

Content Mapping Guides You in Getting the Most Out of Your Content

More content isn't always better. When you solely focus on the amount of content you create, it's likely your content's quality, and relevance suffers. A content map ensures that every piece of content is designed with a purpose and is fully optimized to serve that purpose.

It Helps You Guide Prospective Customers Through the Buying Funnel

Content mapping serves as a guide for reaching your audience swiftly and on the right channel. Your effective content plan should include resources that will engage prospects and nurture them until they're ready to become paying customers.

Get Started with Content Mapping

To follow best practices with your content mapping, you will need:

Comprehension of Business Goals

You know your clients well and what they expect to gain from the content on your website.

Identity of Your Page's Users

You are keenly aware of the material on your site that is useful to your users and why they need to access it.

An Idea of Required Contents

You are aware of the conditions and issues surrounding the materials that you intend to create.

Content Mapping Steps

Steps to follow in creating your content mapping should include:

1. Creating a User or Buyer Persona for Your Audience

To successfully match your target customer's content, you need to know your buyer persona, also referred to as a marketing persona, exceptionally well.

When creating a character, you generalize ideas, characteristics, and even specific demographics. This type of information gives you a clear idea of your recipients on a deeply personal level. Your persona can also include information about age, gender, geography, education level, income, occupation, and interests. When you dig deeper, you can add lifestyle, career goals, concerns, objections, and obstacles. It is a character description that includes needs, pain points, and challenges you can solve with your products or services.

A buyer persona can exude a lasting, positive impact on your company, from engagement with your messages throughout the buying journey to the close of the sale.

Your best customers should provide the most useful, practical insights about your buyer persona. Research those who have been with your company the longest, make repeat purchases, and are most comfortable assisting. Ask yourself:

- What common qualities do these customers possess?

- What made them search for our products or services?

- Why did they purchase our product or service over that of a competitor?

- What goals have they achieved with our products or services?

You might want to consider surveying or interviewing your best customers to find out more about what shaped their experience with your product or service.

When you follow this process, you'll be able to brainstorm better ideas, write human-centered content, promote your content quicker and more efficiently, and increase your conversion rates.

2. Reviewing the Client's Journey and Phases of the Sales Funnel

The customer's experience encompasses all phases that they must go through prior to considering your product or service. This transition includes every stage of the buyer analysis. Here are the main steps in this process:

Awareness

In the recognition stage or **top of the funnel**, your audience realizes their **perceived pains or desired gains.** Problem-aware prospects are looking for informational, useful, valuable content that can help them name their problem and understand it better. Here, the audience begins to realize their concerns, establish their stance, and look for options that meet their goals. This step's appropriate content would include ads on both traditional and digital channels.

Consideration

Your audience is in the **middle of the funnel** or solution-aware phase and possesses the knowledge to define their needs and expectations. They know enough to start reviewing their options, and they are seeking content that connects the dots between their pain and available solutions. Keep in mind that the solutions they're examining aren't necessarily *just* your competitors.

They have completed sufficient research and can discriminate among the various alternatives with a good probability of certainty. The appropriate content for this step would include review sections available on your website, client testimonials, informational landing pages, email push campaigns, blog post reviews, product category pages, resource libraries, eBooks, and FAQs.

Decision

Your audience is now at the **bottom of the funnel** and ready to buy your product or service. Your target audience has completed an in-depth (Step 5) study and conducted comparisons. During this phase, your followers have defined the approach to the solution they require to meet their needs, solve their problems, and eliminate their pain points. They are knowledgeable about their alternatives and set on acting. At this stage, you need to convince your audience that your product or service is their best choice. They need to feel confident that you'll help them resolve their problem, and content exists to drive action and conversion. The compelling content could include pay per clicks (PPCs), email marketing, product tutorials, customer success stories, video training, free courses, landing or opening pages, direct messages to email, coupons, and phone messages such as SMS (or short text message), or app downloads.

3. Establish a Basic Content Marketing Strategy

Use your customer buyer journey map to develop a content marketing strategy. Include what type of content you will publish (blog posts, a video series, checklists, case studies, video interviews, email newsletter, downloadable PDFs, etc.)

Next, think about where you will publish your content (your company blog, standalone website pages, webinar platforms,

YouTube, product knowledge base, Instagram, other social media platforms, etc.)

Then, think about how you will measure results (page views, time on a page, conversion rates, click-throughs, comments, shares, watch time, etc.)

4. Plan Content Topics That Match the Buyer Journey

Approach this step as if it is a game. In 10 minutes, write down as many potential ideas as you can. Use sticky notes. Quantity is the name of this game! Then, in 15 minutes, rank your thoughts on a three-point scale. One is weak, two is average, and three is exceptional. Rank them out loud. Select your best thoughts in another 15 minutes. Your best ideas will rank with the highest scores. Be sure to write these done. You can now move on to the next stage of the game, which involves getting specific about your best ideas.

Ask and answer these simple questions:

- Does this topic address an exact stage of the funnel?
- Does it match a question/problem that my buyer persona has? Does it answer, "What's in it for me?" or the reason your target customer would read it.
- What is the best angle to take with that piece of content?
- What channel or platform should it reach the target customer at the customer journey's ideal point?

After following this exercise, you will have a clear idea of what a piece of content will achieve — and how.

5. *Add Each Content Piece to Your Editorial Calendar*

Give your content pieces life and impact by adding them to your editorial calendar.

A content marketing editorial calendar is a concrete plan for you and your team. It gives you a birds-eye perspective of what's going on and a way to keep everyone organized.

With an editorial content calendar, you'll always know what to prioritize. Here's a simple way to set it up:

    a. Define a deadline for each piece of content. Start with a publishing frequency you can sustain; you can always tweak it later.

    b. Place those pieces on your calendar. A content calendar will help you determine how all your topics sit together and adjust to the time of year or any other circumstances you might have to consider.

    c. Work backward from deadlines to see when pieces need to be researched, written, edited, and prepared for publishing. This strategy is always useful, but particularly for teams that depend on efficient collaboration.

d. Color-code for an accessible overview. With color-coding, you'll quickly see the aim for your buyer persona and funnel stage.

e. Think about how much content you need for every phase of the sales or advertising funnel. Keep the majority of materials content at the top of the funnel, a little less content at the middle of the funnel, and the least amount of content at the funnel's bottom.

6. Establish How to Deliver Each Component of Content

Your content map's final piece is getting the right parts of the content in front of the people needing it most. Without content delivery in the correct channels, you'll waste all the time you've allocated on mapping your content, planning, and construction.

Knowing where to distribute each piece of content, you will need to go back to the notes or tables you created for the funnel's three stages. Conduct an assessment of all the channels you have listed as platforms where your content will live.

Without content distribution, you will waste all the time you've spent on content mapping, brainstorming, planning, and creation.

When planning your content distribution strategy, think about your three funnel stages. Necessary social media works for all sales and marketing funnel stages, but it most easily gains momentum at the top of the funnel. Deliver it here to drive people to a more specific action, such as signing up for a free offer or visiting a particular webpage on your website.

Email marketing is an excellent way to segment subscribers based on their behavior like opens and clicks in the middle and bottom funnels.

Ads on social media are great for all stages of the funnel but in different ways. You can use targeting for the top funnel, including location, employment position, size of the company, age, gender, and similar categories. Be sure to focus on people who have visited specific pages, watched your videos, or otherwise interacted with your content, for those prospects that are lower in the funnel.

And, last but not least, remember your sales and customer service teams. Since they are upfront and personal with your most qualified and interested prospects, pushing them to take that final jump, equip them with middle and bottom-funnel content to deliver it to prospective customers, and close deals more efficiently.

A wise content marketer knows that content promotion doesn't end there. Make sure you consistently explore and test avenues to connect with the right person at the right time — you already have the right pieces of content.

7. Catalog your existing content

Before beginning content mapping, you must be aware of the content you already have. This awareness will prevent you from creating duplicate or redundant content assets.

Perform a content audit and create a catalog of all of your existing content. List each piece of content and details such as:

- Title
- URL
- Category (the theme, topic, or title related to the content)
- Type of content
- Publish date
- Conversion (what you believe will be the next step the audience should take after viewing the content)
- Quality of content

Are There Tools to Create a Content Map?

The content mapping tools you select aren't that important; you could scribble your content maps on paper, a whiteboard, or any form of writing surface you choose. If you need to share your content maps with a team, you can create content maps using web-based tools. There's **OmniGraffle** (for Mac) and, **Basamiq** (for Mac and PC). Or, you can use something as simple as **Microsoft Excel** or even **Word Processing Software.**

There is no reason to make more out of this than necessary for your business. Larger companies with more complex needs might even have a team capable of doing this. For smaller firms, content maps, although very important in your company's overall marketing strategy, can be paired down to a content map that is quite simple. The important thing is to DO it. Your content map should include:

- A notion, even if it's a rough idea, for the content you need to produce and the existing content you already have at your disposal.
- Labels for your content, including FAQ, white papers, etc.

Getting the Most from Your Content Maps
- Compel folks to see them

- As your followers see your content maps, these will aid them in getting a clearer picture of your content. This will then lead to getting better feedback on the content itself.

Using Maps to Aid in Tech Decisions

You can make better technology decisions, including what publishing platform to select, when you see what content will be published.

Maintaining Updated Concept Maps

You must constantly update your concept maps. After all, it's unreasonable to think they won't need any changes at all. Your maps should be modified to suit the new developments in your processes. They should also change as your site changes. If your company also shifts goals and targets, your concept maps should also reflect this.

Maintaining Your Content Maps Neat

To organize completed concept maps, project management tools can help you make this task easier. For instance, tools such as **Basecamp** or **Asana** can get the job done very well.

Post-Purchase Materials

Although it is not part of content mapping, businesses need to remember that post-Purchase content supports customers after their purchase and re-engages and remarkets to them to bring them back into the purchase funnel. After all, content marketing must continue long after your close the deal and secure your customer. You want to be sure to keep your customer and not lose them. Without ongoing contact, with most achievable through additional content, you are likely to lose that customer.

Post-purchase content continues to support **customer lifecycle marketing** and should include:

- o User guides
- o Customer-specific portals
- o Email newsletters
- o Coupons
- o Surveys
- o Social media posts

In conclusion, content mapping is a powerful tool for content marketing and an essential part of a strategic content plan. With a content map in place, you can review your existing content materials, plan for new content, and determine how each asset will be applied to reach and engage your target audience effectively.

Your content plan is more efficient and effective at engaging your audience when you visualize the content you need to shepherd prospective customers through your sales funnel. A clearly defined user depiction (or client profile) enables you to drill down to determine your audience's needs and expectations. Once you have uncovered your target audience, you will be able to determine where they lie in the customer's process. This insight will allow you to produce a plan leading to quality materials.

Regardless of demographics, audience member moves through the path to reach the moment of acquiring your products and services. When you go about to work on content mapping, you can align your content with your audience's desires and expectations to create a lasting relationship.

Simply put, content mapping is a simple exercise that will pay off for months and years to come.

Chapter 6: Step 6 - Appeal to Your Customer-Base

In previous chapters, we reviewed what content marketing is, building the story, content marketing benefits, building and strategizing your content marketing campaign, and creating and using content mapping.

In this chapter, we will cover the "how-to" appeal to your customer with the right content. Would they prefer visual content or information to build knowledge, in-depth articles, emails, Facebook, or video content?

A perfect world for content marketers would exist if each new person to your site got your product or service. We don't mean later, right now, and on your website.

Not likely. What's more plausible is that after navigating your complex sales funnel, they *might* make a purchase.

Without channeling negative vibes, we have to realize that selling isn't easy. It is more difficult today due to a more sophisticated customer, and access to information about you and your competitor's deals more readily than ever before.

Research validates that the average customer engages with three to five content items prior to talking to a sales representative, and 87 percent of prospective buyers go about their due diligence through digital means.

So, as emphasized in previous chapters, the proper materials will get their focus. Since customers nowadays are quite savvy, they cross-reference various content items throughout various channels before going along the three sales funnels on their purchasing journey.

Finding the most specific content to provide answers to your customer's questions, cultivate positive perception and connection with you, and over the long haul, transform leads into loyal customers is quite the feat. This is so complex that most companies and advertisers don't have clear ideas on what the best type of content should be.

How Much and How Often

When trying to navigate the complex landscape of the right content, some questions might include:

- How many blog posts should I write?
- Should I tweet daily?
- How much should I allocate to video in my content marketing plan?
- Does my company need white papers and e-books?

A Simple Framework to Follow

A great content strategy should resemble more of a Q&A. For instance, research what questions your customers are asking and then provide detailed answers to create trust and move customers closer to interacting with your brand.

Following this simple framework allows you to see each content item as you build instances to draw customers closer to a new sale, or to compel them to act. Content synergy is a crucial component in this aspect. It is pointless to produce unlimited amounts of content if your followers don't interact with it at one point or another.

If you have a hard time developing relevant and interesting content, seek new means of updating your current materials, or find new content items to hone in on other parts of the funnel, this chapter will discuss how effective content marketing approach may be created.

The Content Marketing Funnel

This type of funnel consists of a methodology in which you can get as many leads as you can, so they go through a clearly delineated procedure that transforms them into paying customers for your company.

At the largest portion, the **top** part of this funnel, a considerable quantity of potential customers might be keen on your products or services. This large number makes up your prospects, that is, possible customers.

As your prospective customers go through the line towards the **middle**, the majority will go by the wayside through a much narrower neck. Finally, a reduced quantity of leads will get through to the bottom of the **funnel,** thereby becoming customers.

Where Does Each Type of Content Go?

This is a profound question that all advertising professional seeks to respond to:

What type of content should be used at each stage?

So, let's take a look at the content marking funnel broken down into its three stages along with sample content for each one of the stages:

- **Top Funnel or Aware**
    - Ads
    - Checklists
    - Infographics
    - Landing pages
    - Videos

- **Middle Funnel or Engage**
  - o Blog posts (How-To Guides)
  - o Social Media
  - o White papers/E-books
  - o Case Studies
  - o Webinars
  - o Ratings & Client testimonies
  - o Emails

- **Bottom-Funnel or Thrill (Customer)**
  - o Special offers
  - o Emails
  - o Social Media

Of course, these are ideas for best practices; however, a company's specific sales cycle, industry type, and audience create the final content type choices for each funnel stage. These ideas *do* hold constant for a lot of companies that show effective advertising campaigns.

As such, let's take a look at the type of materials and review the reasons why it's successful at its corresponding step of the funnel.

1. *Content for Attracting Leads Ads*

Running ads is an effective way to quickly increase your site's traffic, and they are at **the top of the funnel**. Both are fantastic ways to place your name in front of your followers. Statistics inform us that for every $1 spent on Google Ads, businesses earn an average sale of $2, and research further validates that overall social ad spending is increasing. To unearth your audience and which content approach is best suited for them, you will have a little upfront monetary outlay.

2. *Search Ads*

On social platforms, your target audiences are not necessarily interested in buying, but rather to be entertained with funny pictures and videos, catch up with friends, etc. So, to grab the attention your way, you need to push your way into their attention with something that stands out. It needs to stand out and show something different. Examples include ads on Facebook and Instagram. An excellent example is Air Asia https://www.facebook.com/AirAsia/posts/10156375652257387.

In 2018, Air Asia created a static-image promo that screams "simplicity" but ticks off all the practical ad boxes. The copy, "Free Seats," 5 million Promo Seats, uses few words. The bright graphic on a fiery red background might suffice to stop scrollers from moving forward, as words such as "FREE" or "limited time offer" can be used as powerful calls to action.

3. Landing Pages

When you run paid ads, you will send your viewers to your website's landing page. Well-written landing page content can help massively increase conversions. Maintain a consistent message. Identify the most important aspect you want to transmit so you can build your content around it. Please keep it simple with consistent white space than text. Stick to one angle. Perhaps it's the customer's financial savings, such as free shipping or an extended money-back guarantee, or a discount. Offers like these are a fabulous way to turn that procrastinating lead into a paying customer. And these offers are great for filling the **top of the funnel.** Further down on the landing page, there could be a link to a clearer sales site offering greater advantages for acquiring any of your products.

4. Video

The need to communicate considerable information for unqualified prospects at the **top of the funnel**, that are unfamiliar with your brand, videos content is quite useful. Since unqualified prospects are either unfamiliar with your brand or have never had the chance to interact with your products, you must capture their focus with compelling, introductory material. Video has a positive reputation for producing higher search engine optimization and more vigorous engagement. Statistics show that 84 percent of consumers purchase an item because of a convincing product showcase. What is even more impressive is by 2022, the video platform will dominate 83 percent of all Internet traffic.

When you add a video to your website opening page, you can boost conversions at a rate greater than 80 percent. Since video is also suitable for mobile devices, you are in front of 5.1 billion unique mobile users worldwide.

As a bonus, not to be missed, be sure to share the videos to create abundant material for your YouTube and Instagram profiles.

Videos are a tangible way to take advantage of people's preferences for mobile media. That way, you can capture new prospects and draw them to your brand. Also, repurpose video content in spots throughout your website, blogs, and hot links in e-newsletters.

5. *Infographics*

Creating and using an infographic is a great means of attracting attention, boosting backlinks, and achieving a comfortable social media presence. Research informs us that people love stats relevant to their industry, mainly if presented in a bite-size style, and when used in this way, infographics can profoundly affect your marketing at the **top of the funnel**.

Proven stats indicate that more than 65 percent of advertisers utilize infographics for the purpose of marketing primarily because people absorb images and "chunks" of text 60,000 times faster than rich content and retain the data for more than three days.

Infographics demonstrate impressive results and perform better on social media. More than 40 percent of content developers report that original graphics engage a prospect better than purely textual content.

Although not new, infographics are a great addition to your advertising mix, especially if you're presenting information that requires visualization. They are a great tool when information, imagery, and layout are needed to display data in an easily digestible way that might otherwise be stale and unattractive.

6. *Checklists*

Folks found at the uppermost **portion of the funnel** require a solution to a conflict they face. They are not in a place where they are looking for an actual product or service. At this point, they are searching for ways and things to solve their problem. A particular product or service is not yet a clear vision for a prospect.

To snatch their attention, you need to remove your focus from the sale and refocus on how you can help your prospect fix their issue.

Thus, a good checklist can provide your prospective customer with a structured procedure to achieve this. If you can assist them, they will be more willing to keep your brand in mind every time they need to purchase.

The catch is that after potential customer reviews and use your checklist; you want them to come back. An innovative way to achieve this is to include a free checklist that calls for an email address. In doing so, you capture the data for your mailing list, and you give your viewers contact details for their future follow-up. Checklists, with a "catch," accomplish this.

7. *How-to Blog Posts*

Once your prospects have hit your landing page, found you on social media, consumed your video content, and compelling infographics. Now, you have to give them more.

When a prospect decides your product or service may be useful, they question your brand's validity. You can accomplish this by establishing yourself as a thought leader. Valuable leaders, with the knowledge to convey, offer free advice. The most concise way to meet this goal is through a blog or "how-to" posted on your blog or website.

8. *Social media*

Reaching a respectable level of vital traffic on Google takes time. As a successful content marketer, you can't just sit around and wait for your target audience to discover your content. You have to act. That's where social media comes in at **the middle and bottom of the funnel**. Social media is a perfect means of attracting prospective customers with a wickedly brilliant pitch to capture their focus.

Reliable evidence shows us that 97 percent of marketers use social media to reach their audience, and 65 percent of sales professionals use social selling to fill their pipeline.

Social media claims an estimated 2.77 billion global participants. This is why it's quite simple to see the reach social media has. Through the creation of frequent, updated, and consistent means through these platforms, it is possible to provide prospects with access to your expertise. In doing so, you provide them with the opportunity to see what current customers have to say. A potential customer can automatically go through any number of catchy pictures, posts, and other comments by happy consumers. It is the fastest, more secure means of attracting prospective customers to reach them consistently.

A solid social media strategy must include regular updates to every social media profile for your business so that you can keep a constant and robust position while serving your customers' needs.

Social is great for attracting new leads and interacting with your potential customers a little further down the funnel while fostering a much close relationship.

9. Case Studies

Case studies provide another wonderful chance to build your credibility and clear leadership roles are with case studies in the **middle of the funnel**. After all, they emphasize that your company is an expert in your chosen field.

Case studies aren't simply a means of catching interested people's focus. It is a way of fostering a strong relationship with those folks seeking your content.

10. White Papers/E-Books

There are times when a blog post isn't sufficient to convert that prospect into a sale. Maybe you need to offer more specifics and in-depth content on the topic to demonstrate your expertise in your industry. That's why a white paper or e-book can help. Interested parties can then transition toward the **middle of the funnel** by receiving more in-depth materials.

Research informs us that 75 percent of buyers indicate they would share information from a white paper, and 71 percent utilize information from white papers to determine purchasing matters.

Leads with more invested in the funnel tend to prefer the longer-form content, such as a white paper or e-book. To close the sale, you have to demonstrate your authority further. When this type of lead is prepared to offer their email in exchange for the information you have to offer. This is a crucial step in building your funnel.

11. Webinars

You can always capture attention with video however webinars can take that concept to the next level. Instead of merely showing a video of your pre-recorded materials, you can use it to display your knowledge or expertise. As such, a webinar, or an online workshop, can be conducted in real-time with real people.

Evidence shows that 93 percent of webinar participants enjoy asking questions at the end of a webinar. Sixty percent of marketers use webinars, which apply to **the funnel's middle**, as part of their content marketing strategy. When you demonstrate your knowledge through webinars, they are an innovative way to engage interested, potential customers before influencing them toward a purchase decision. Webinars are one of the best tools to hook new leads and teach people hands-on methods to see success.

12. Ratings and Client Testimonials

When looking to engage prospective customers, testimonials from existing customers can provide you with credible feedback. However, it is important to note that we're not talking about fake testimonials claiming miraculous results. Whenever possible, please get real people who are willing to lend their names and comments. In this manner, you can show your prospective leads that you are the real deal.

There is one catch though. Please try to avoid offering incentives for positive comments. Ideally, these folks should provide their positive comments because they genuinely feel you have done a good job.

13. Emails

Though some advertisers feel that email is old school, it is still one of the most effective ways that you can engage with your audience. The fact is that email is the easiest and most accessible way to reach both customers and prospects.

Perhaps the biggest advantage that email offers is automation. You don't need to manually set up posts and contents like on social media. On social media, you need to create content, post it, and then maintain it. This is something that you don't need to do with email.

Email is also a great way of segmenting and targeting specific audiences. You can go about this segmentation through a simple email opt-in on your website or social media platforms. Also, you segment by posting on forums or other types of online spaces.

The content you put out via email should provide customers with quick and easy information they can gobble up. Long-form posts and materials would best be saved for an e-book or white paper. You can also redirect your users to YouTube or a blog. As such, your aim should be the maintain constant communication with your audience.

This tactic is simply a means of moving leads through the pipeline. You shouldn't expect to make any conversions at this point. You should expect to use email to entice people to get on your channels and keep the funnel moving.

14. Special Offers and Loyalty Programs

Loyalty programs are a way of retaining customers. After all, once a customer has purchased from you, you want to make sure they keep coming back. Unless you have the type of product or service that can only be purchased once, you want customers to keep coming back as much as possible.

On the whole, roughly 80% of customers look for some kind of reward or loyalty program as an incentive to keep coming back. This is where companies produce member-only exclusives or special offers available only to returning customers.

Several large corporations use loyalty and reward schemes to help retain their customers. These schemes include points for frequent purchases, special promotional gear, and even discounts available to returning customers. One of the most successful loyalty schemes is hiking up the price of new customers. So, returning customers feel they are getting a better deal than new ones.

Consequently, loyalty programs and schemes provide customers with a specific sense of belonging. It makes them feel like they have a good sense of what the customers want and how they can keep them coming back for more.

Here are some pointers to consider when it comes to generating loyalty among customers.

- Great experiences foster positive feelings among customers. Thus, satisfied customers generally become unofficial brand ambassadors. They will gladly share a positive experience with their friends and family. On the contrary, negative experience automatically leads to bad press.
- With modern technology, the internet offers quick and easy access to all sorts of information. In this regard, customers can find information on your products and

services readily available. Therefore, customers use these tools to move along the sales cycle at their pace.

- Ultimately, the point is to increase sales and revenues. This leads to moving things along the sales funnel. When all strategies are executed properly, you can ensure that the cycle will get easier as the process moves along.

Lastly, please keep in mind that maintaining a healthy sales pipeline is something critical to all businesses. Regardless of size, all companies need to make sure their sales funnel is constantly filling up. Whether it's returning customers or brand-new ones, increasing sales is always the goal. Please remember that it's always cheaper to retain customers than it is to attract new ones. So, make sure that you have your game plan in order. It will save you lots of time and headaches down the road.

Chapter 7: Step 7 - Distributing Your Content

Once you have the right content up and running, your attention should shift to distributing your content in the most effective manner possible. Just like your products, efficient distribution will lead to increased sales. After all, if you can deliver your products in a timely way, customers will have no issue accessing them. The same goes for your materials. If you deliver in a timely fashion, your customers will have everything they need, when they need it.

One of the biggest mistakes that advertisers make is to produce great plans but fail to deliver on them. Making great plans is only half of the battle. The other half of the battle is to make sure you follow through on everything you set out to accomplish. Otherwise, you'll miss great opportunities to deliver on the content your audience can fully take advantage of.

Effective content distribution is a crucial element of any successful marketing plan. In this chapter, we are going to take a look at how you can produce great plans that will lead you to achieve your goals. So, we'll be talking about how you can build a distribution plan that will be effective for you. The most important thing to keep in mind is your audience's preferred channels. These are the channels that you need to focus on.

Content Distribution Process

In essence, content distribution is a process that comprises the sharing, dissemination, or publication of materials. In other words, it is the process by which your content is made available to audiences across various platforms and media.

Nowadays, there are a plethora of channels to choose from. In addition to traditional media (print, radio, television), there are plenty of digital channels such as social media, video, and text. In a way, these channels are a type of digitalization of traditional media. Regardless of the media used, distribution happens only after content is produced. As such, thinking about distribution before content production is like putting the cart before the horse.

It is key to know where and how you figure you will disseminate your materials. That way, you can keep this in mind as you produce your content. Without a good idea of how you plan to distribute your materials, you may produce content that isn't quite suitable later on.

Here are some things to consider when thinking about your distribution strategy.

- 60% of marketers create one piece of content daily
- 8,726 tweets posted on Twitter each second
- 952 Instagram posts per second
- Google answers almost four million search queries per minute

An important thing to keep in mind here is that you need to match your content to your distribution channels. When you keep these elements in mind, you can produce materials to suit your channels effectively.

Content Distribution Channels

In short, these are the media you plan to utilize to disseminate your content. These could be traditional or digital. The main aspect here is to ensure that you have the right type of materials for your intended channel.

Owned Content Distribution

Owned distribution refers to the digital assets that your company actually owns. For example, a blog or website are good examples. Social media platforms are not as your company does not own them outright.

Earned Content Distribution

There are third-party channels that are free to access. For instance, social media platforms, video sharing, and email servers constitute "earned content." Consequently, your company may use them free or pay for access to them.

Paid Content Distribution

These are specific content distribution that requires some type of payment for their use. There are plenty of such platforms and media.

This depends on the type of audience you are looking to reach. The most common paid distribution are ads on search engines, videos on platforms such as YouTube, and sponsored posts on social media.

Pay-Per-Click (PPC) Ads

These types of ads cost a specific amount of money every time a customer clicks on one of the ads. Most PPC campaigns cost pennies per click. Naturally, if an ad gets thousands of clicks, this will represent thousands to be paid. Of course, thousands of clicks would also hopefully represent a high volume of sales.

Sponsored Content

Sponsored content constitutes any type of content that you pay to display. These ads range from social media posts, videos, or text. Most social media platforms live off sponsored content. These platforms put their analytics at the service of advertisers. That's how you can leverage social media to target the customers you want to reach.

Paid Influencer Content

Influencers are well-known individuals that have a large following. As such, they can reach a large number of people with every post, video, or content they share. Hence, brands reach out to them so they can promote their products. In some cases, influencers simply get free gear. Other times, brands will offer a monetary incentive. These payments may vary. Still, any brand can virtually reach out to these folks at any time.

Paid Social Ads

These can include PPCs or pay-per-click, endorsed, or influencer content. Paid social media ads can be successful for marketing messages by way of social media sites like **Facebook**, **LinkedIn**, and **Instagram** while earmarking secondary audiences on these sites, too.

Pay-per-click ads (PPCs) are the type of marketing tactics that create an ad in which users click on it. Once they click, they are redirected to another page or site that contains information on the brand of the product. Often, these ads can be found on social media sites.

Content Distribution Plan

Content is not all created equally. Therefore, each type typically requires a content distribution plan. Here are several content marketing materials and suggestions for distribution channels.

E-books

Distribute your e-book content by way of a gated form located on a landing page, so you can capture contact information or answer a low-friction question.

An example is **HubSpot's** landing page. On this page, users can provide their data so they can obtain access to each e-book. Channels to post e-books include:

- o **blog.reedsy.com**
- o **Fivvr.com**
- o **onlinebookclub.org**
- o **pubby. co**
- o **scribewriting.com**
- o **taboola.com**

Podcasts and Interviews

Apple Podcasts, **Spotify**, or **Google Podcasts** are great platforms to distribute your podcasts or interview content. Another example of a suitable venue is **HubSpot's Weird Work podcast**, which links to and is available on all three podcast networks in addition to **SoundCloud.**

Buzzsprout.com, www.audry.io, itunes.com, **buffer.com** are other channels for your podcasts and interview. You can also pin your episode tweet or **Facebook** post, featuring the **iTunes URL**.

Press Releases

By using **press releases** to support your overall **content marketing** strategy, you help your brand gain visibility, build authority, improve search rankings, and reach journalists who act as your conduit to a new, broader audience. **PR Newswire,** a press release distribution network, helps you target and contact journalists and outlets by industry, geographic areas, and topics. State and local, regional, and national press contacts are available as well. **HARO** stands for Help a Reporter Out. It is an online platform that connects journalists and sources. For this book, you would be the source. **HARO** sends you daily emails with journalist queries, and when you respond to these queries, your business may be the recipient of a feature article. HARO is a reactive content distribution tool, but it helps get press mentions and backlinks.

Print Publications

Although digital media has a strong presence and place in content marketing, let's not underestimate print publications' value. Print extends the opportunity to create something uncommon in today's digital world and stand out in an overcrowded market of branded content. You might want to consider making a subscription-based connection to consumers about topics that educate, retain, and increase brand loyalty. There has never been a more incredible opportunity for brands in the print publications channel than right now.

So, as your business devotes more revenue to its content marketing budget, ask yourself how you can get the most out of incorporating print into your content marketing plan? The key is to produce a high niche and targeted publication that positions your business as a top expert on your audience's subject matter.

As with any content marketing strategy, you want to tie your print content to the content you create for your other channels. You most definitely want an online counterpart to your print publication. Your tactic could include a landing page on your business website or even a dedicated website where you make your print content available for digital consumption.

Videos

You can distribute your video content through **YouTube** or **Video.** Another example is **HubSpot's YouTube channel**, which shares brand content, how-to videos, and written content in a video format. **Other free video-sharing channels are:**

- o **Break.com**
- o **Dailymotion.com**
- o **LiveLeak.com**
- o **Metacafe.com**
- o **Twitch.com**
- o **Vimeo.com**

Infographics

An excellent channel to distribute your infographic content is on **Pinterest**, as well as on your blog. Be sure to include your infographics in your **white papers** as well. For other channels to promote your infographics, look into:

- **Amazing infographics**
- **Cool Infographics**
- **Daily Infographic**
- **Flickr**
- **I Love Charts**
- **Infographaolic**
- **Infographic Bee**
- **Infographic Labs**
- **Mashable Infographics**
- **News I Like**
- **Reddit**
- **SlideShare**
- **Visual.ly**
- **Infographic Review**
- **Fast Company**
- **Flowing Data**
- **Infographic Journal**
- **Infographics Showcase**
- **Media Caffeine**
- **NerdGraph**

Case Studies and Success Stories

An appropriate location to make your case studies and success stories accessible is a dedicated page on your **website, newsletters,** other **publications,** and **social media,** particularly **Facebook.** Also, consider **HubSpot's Case Studies page,** where visitors have access to all types of case studies featuring **HubSpot** customers. Other suitable channels to post case studies and success stories are **LinkedIn Publisher,** answer a question on **Quora,** attach your case study, or turn your case study into a **SlideShare** presentation. Also, post your case study in **industry-specific** **forums** and **social networks, email** case studies to prospects, and marketing lists.

Webinars

There are several ways to distribute your webinar content:

- o Through a **dedicated and optimized webinar page on your website**
- o As announcements at the end of your blog posts and articles
- o added as a **call-to-action**
- o or create **a simple teaser video on YouTube**
- o Promote your upcoming webinar in **your email signatures** as a save-the-date
- o Add it to your **thank you pages**
- o **Post it to webinar listing sites** such as **tellonline.org** and **webinarbase.com**, which are both free

o Distribute your webinar content through **HubSpot's Webinars webpage,** where visitors can also browse and access free webinar content

Email Signatures

WiseStamp, an email tool that allows you (and your employees) to share your latest content in your email signature, is an essential piece of owned real estate that will be visible every time someone opens your email. **WiseStamp** can assist you in taking advantage of that space. Additionally, every email service provider offers the ability to set up an email signature, including uploading artwork, other graphics, and customizable content.

Blogs

Many companies publish all of their content on their blog and then repurpose and re-publish it through various content channels. Blog posts read globally are easy to repurpose, translate into other languages, and simple to share — not to mention that almost 50 percent of consumers read blogs while executing purchase decisions. That's the reason we encourage building a business blog and then expanding your content types to publicize on other channels. You can also guest post on other blogs, add blog posts to printed newsletters, magazines, e-zines, and forums. You might also want to consider distributing a daily or weekly e-newsletter to your email list with a synopsis of your best or recent content.

HubSpot Blog is perfect for posting your blog to other locations. Other channels for posting blogs include:

- o **BizSugar**
- o **Blogpros.com**
- o **Facebook Groups**
- o **Flipboard**
- o **Instagram**
- o **LinkedIn Pulse**
- o **Medium**
- o **Pinterest**
- o **Pocket**
- o **Quuu Promote**
- o **Reddit**
- o **Squarespace.com**
- o **Vimeo**
- o **Wix.com**
- o **YouTube**
- o **Amazon, iTunes**
- o **Dzone**
- o **Google web search**
- o **Google+**
- o **Managewp.org**
- o **Tumblr**
- o **Twitter**
- o **Yahoo Answers**

Make Smart Channel Choices

You may post on forums, and other channels discussed — and pay to promote your content on those sites, too. Alternatively, you may choose to share content exclusively on social media channels, or perhaps you find that traditional public relations are your best choice.

Whatever content distribution channels you opt for, make sure they band together with your audience's predispositions and responses. Be sure to attend to your owned distribution channels — your blog, public website and Intranet, newsletters, and social media profiles — since these are inexpensive and within your domain of owned properties and reflect your brand, service, or product. It is easier to control the stream of information on a channel you control while also serving as your home base for the influx your content precipitates.

Once you construct a possible audience of captivated acolytes, you can broaden your scope to include other channels to spur more traffic in your direction and enlarge and enhance the audience's experience with your brand.

While following your editorial calendar and selected distribution channels, publish and market your new content. Be sure to follow the rules

to optimize your posts on each channel. Regardless of the amount of care, attention, and time you dedicate to building your content strategy and crafting persuasive, engaging copy, your brand's potential for success often lives or dies by your distribution and promotion choices.

Quite a few brands make the mistake of posting their content anywhere and everywhere to increase the probability of attaining the desired results. The challenge with plastering your content without any discerning rationale is that you are highly unlikely to reach the right audience, whether those circles are receptive to your messages or whether the audience relationships built there solidify a meaningful impact on your business.

In conclusion, your content distribution channels are arguably more important than your content itself. Great content is a loss if no one is devouring it. Content dissemination is a crucial part of the content marketing puzzle. It's is also the master key to boosting your brand awareness, attracting loyal followers, and encouraging your readers to click, act, and transform into customers.

In conclusion, there are so many content channels at your fingertips to spread your brand's value globally; there's no justification for letting your best assets wither and die on the vine. Distribute your content using good judgment and promote it conscientiously, and your brand will enjoy a high performance from every piece of content you create.

Conclusion

Content marketing can be a crucial cog in building a thriving, tenable business, and this guide covered why content marketing is vital for any modern business entity. Whether it's developing great, memorable content ideas to conceptualizing marketing funnels that metamorphose newcomers into customers, this guide covered it all.

Through a seven-step approach, this "how-to" guide allowed you to get inside the mind of your target audience and create a rich audience experience for your business, current, and future clients and learn how to build content that completely captivates, intrigues, and engages your audience. Readers also discover what channels to use to successfully promote content, based on finding influencers interested in your content, leveraging a content marketing strategy for better visibility, credibility, increased sales, and understanding the rationale of a content marketing process.

You were also introduced to the myriad ways you can succeed with content marketing, how to wire together blogs, offers, outreach, metrics, and more to build a content marketing system that will systematically improve over time. Additionally, readers will learn how to create customer personas to improve how you create content that guides your ideal customer and manage a content creation calendar.

Learning about the "soft" benefits of content marketing: public trust, more engaged prospects, and happier clients is an added feature.

With the information you have uncovered in this guide, you will find that it is quite easy to make the most of your opportunities to hit the mark with your customers. So, don't waste any time. Now is the perfect moment to make the most of everything you have always wanted to achieve. With content marketing, you are well on your way to making the most of your company's value proposition.

More by Santino Spencer

Discover all books from the Marketing Management Series by
Santino Spencer at:

bit.ly/santino-spencer

Book 1: Marketing Strategy

Book 2: Business Branding

Book 3: Digital Marketing

Book 4: Social Media Marketing

Book 5: Marketing Analytics

Book 6: Content Marketing

Book 7: Business Development

Book 8: Mobile Marketing

Themed book bundles available at discounted prices:

bit.ly/santino-spencer